The MYSTICAL LAWS

GOING BEYOND THE DIMENSIONAL BOUNDARIES

RYUHO OKAWA

IRH Press

Contents

Preface 11

⌁ CHAPTER ONE ⌁

Life after Death

~ Life Is Not Limited to This World ~

CHAPTER TWO

The Principle of Spiritual Possession

~ How to Protect Yourself from Evil Spirits ~

CHAPTER THREE

The Principle of Channeling

~ For Receiving and Spreading Light ~

ᴄᴏ CHAPTER FOUR ᴄᴏ

Occultism as Power
~ Release the Power Bound by The Commonly Accepted Knowledge ~

ᨆCHAPTER FIVEᨆ

What it Means to Believe

~ Go Beyond the Boundaries between This World and the Next ~

Preface

Within an hour of reading this book, all that you have accepted as common knowledge will crumble away. Indeed, no school or mass media has ever taught you the truth. Whatever doubts you may have, this book will reveal the truths of the great universe.

As the author, I will refrain from saying too much in the preface. I will simply present you with this book, the tenth in the Laws series.

Ryuho Okawa
Founder and CEO of Happy Science Group
Autumn 2004

Chapter One

Life after Death

~ Life is Not Limited to this World ~

Lecture given on May 18, 2003

1

A Knowledge of "Life after Death" Will Change Your Way of Life

I would like to start this book with the subject of "life after death." On hearing this title, you may think of words such as *soul* or *spirit*, but I will speak on "life after death" in general. I often talk about the world of higher dimensions in a logical way, as if it is an accepted fact. This sometimes puts off people who do not believe in the other world and who tend to distance themselves from religion. Therefore, in this chapter, I would like to write on the subject in a way that is acceptable even to beginners.

How do people generally think about life after death? I suppose many people wish that it existed, but, at the same time, they do not fully believe in it because there is no solid proof of its existence. Educational textbooks do not touch on this subject and most schools merely teach that life was formed through the random evolution of small clumps of protein. Although medical science studies in many ways how to deal with the period just before death, when it comes to the world after death, most people avoid thinking about it and do not even want to know about it. So the concept of what happens after death lies outside the boundaries of education.

In a sense, however, knowing about life after death is vital in life. For instance, even if you have little knowledge of different subjects of this world, you must at least know the truth about whether or not life continues in the other world after death. Unless you know this single truth, you will have a completely different understanding of your life in this world.

If life were limited only to this world and everything ended with death, then people could live accordingly, but if another world exists after death, as the old tales say, then it is necessary to live in the appropriate way. Whether or not you believe in the existence of life after death will greatly affect the way you live. Therefore this is an extremely important subject and the knowledge of life after death is valuable in a way that cannot be compared with any other knowledge.

In olden times, "life after death" was the main subject of philosophy, but many philosophers could not stand the doubt about its existence because they were unable to prove it and gradually moved on to discussing more abstract ideologies. Today, philosophy has changed into something unrelated to the world after death, becoming more akin to logic. As a result, philosophy has moved away from the subject of the world after death.

A religion cannot be called a religion if it does not teach about the afterworld, but over time Buddhism has become interpreted as a form of materialism. In the same way, philosophy has moved away from discussing this world and the next, to more abstract subjects. Even if philosophers or religious people initially teach about the next world, as time passes, people with no spiritual experience or belief in the other world misinterpret the teachings and pass them on in a different way.

2

My Spiritual Experiences

Many people undergo spiritual experiences

People who believe in the other world may imagine that the true form of a human being is a human-shaped spirit dwelling inside a physical body. They may believe that after the physical body is buried or cremated, the spirit will remain on Earth for some time before being led to the next world, where it begins a new life. Usually, people have only a vague idea of what happens after that, and just think that they will find out after they die.

I am sure all of you have heard at least one or two ghost stories. But because modern society tends to deny the existence of the other world academically and is dominated by the supremacy of science, people avoid sharing their spiritual experiences. They often put these down to delusion, illusion, or hallucination and keep quiet. If, however, they were to ask not just their immediate family, but also more distant relatives, they would find that there are others who have also undergone spiritual experiences.

Up until World War II, people in Japan were more religious and it was much easier to discuss spiritual phenomena, but nowadays this sort of subject is mostly limited to a certain type of television program. This makes us believe that spiritual experiences are rarer these days, but there are still many people who have this kind of experience.

Spirits of a writer and an actor
Who visited me after death

I would now like to offer some examples of the spiritual experiences I have undergone. There was a famous Japanese novelist, T. K., who was a member of Happy Science and was also a holder of a Happy Science Headquarters lectureship. After he died several years ago, his spirit visited me sometimes. His death was so sudden that he was unable to prepare himself for it and he was in and out of my home for two or three months until he finally returned to the other world.

There was also a Japanese actor, K. N., who used to hold the same title of lecturer at Happy Science. He too came to visit me the day after he died. I usually avoid meeting the spirits of ordinary people, but if it is somebody who used to be active as our headquarters lectureship and who has talked to me in person while still alive, I cannot always avoid them. So I talked to them as an unavoidable duty, like paying taxes, until they were satisfied.

These kinds of people have a good understanding of Buddha's Truth, so they are not such scary beings, but if they stay near me for too long, it interferes with my daily life. So when the spirit of K. N. turned up at my home, I hoped he wouldn't stay for too long. I said to him, "I would be grateful if you do not stay as long as T. K. did, but limit your visit to just two or three days." We talked together for some time and soon he returned to the other world.

The place where I live is protected by a spiritual screen that generally prevents evil spirits or the spirits of the dead from entering. Many people die every day from traffic accidents or illnesses and if I allowed everybody's souls to visit me, I would never have time for anything else. That is why I create a barrier around my home, preventing spirits from seeing me. The barrier is not as big as Tokyo Dome, but is shaped like a dome or a tent.

In the case of my relative's death, if the person has a deep connection to Buddha's Laws, he or she is able to visit me after he or she dies, but other people cannot even see where I am. The spirits are unable to see me, so they cannot gain access to my house.

When their vibration is attuned, spirits can visit Even through literature or music

As I have explained, I am surrounded by a spiritual screen that generally prevents spirits from visiting me, but there are exceptions when I attune my mind to that of a spirit. When our thoughts connect with each other's, we can meet.

For example, when I see an obituary in the newspaper with a photograph of the dead person and if it is somebody I know, I'll naturally think of that person. Then my mind will attune to that person's mind and, usually within two or three seconds, his or her spirit will come to my side as expected. Just as in the Spirit World, spirits can move very quickly.

Sometimes when I am watching the news on television, if I am not careful, the same thing happens. For this reason, I try not to look too closely at reports of people's deaths on television, and only listen with half an ear. The same is true for the obituary column in the newspapers.

I must be careful with books as well. Many authors of the books that are available today are already dead and if I suspect that the author has gone to Hell, I would rather avoid reading his or her work. That is because, simply by me reading a book, the spirit of the author will come to visit me. This is quite hard to bear.

As I read a book by somebody who is already dead, my mind starts attuning to the vibrations the author emitted when he or she was alive, and this opens the way for the spirit to come. Therefore, after awakening spiritually, no matter how well known a book or how famous its author, I first look at their views on life and the way in which they died and if I suspect that they have fallen to Hell, I refrain from reading their work.

It isn't much of a problem if the spirit soon returns home, but if it stays for a while, it will affect my life. If it were to come every evening for a month or so, and stay until late, it would make my life difficult. It may be unable to return to Heaven for various reasons, but if it decides to stick around me since it has nowhere else to go, it will distract me from my work. This is a serious problem because, although it may have nothing better to do, I have many important tasks. For these reasons, if I think a book comes from a dangerous source, I do not read it.

A great number of literature works are hellish in their content. People may find them interesting because the stories or the graphic descriptions in this hellish literature are very close to life on Earth and are familiar to people living in this world. Seen from a spiritual viewpoint, however, this is extremely frightening.

In this way, although I generally remain invisible to spirits because of the spiritual screen, if my mind becomes attuned to that of a spirit, that spirit will be able to track me down. It is as if they had my telephone or fax number, and they are able to contact me.

I have explained how a spirit can come to me when I read a book. The same is true of music. There is a piece by Richard Strauss [1864-1949] entitled "Also

Sprach Zarathustra," and when I listened to this one day, the spirit of Nietzsche, the German philosopher [1844–1900] who wrote a book of the same title, appeared from out of Hell. I think that when Strauss wrote that piece, he must have been thinking about Nietzsche's work. That is why when I listened to the music, Nietzsche's spirit appeared. I felt an evil vibration and it put me off from ever listening to the piece again.

When I told people about this, they were very surprised that such phenomena could happen, but spirits will indeed come to me when I am listening to their music. So listening to a piece of music alone opens the way for a spirit to come, because as you listen to the music for ten or twenty minutes, your consciousness becomes attuned to its frequency.

In the Spirit World, you cannot see spirits You are not interested in

When some connection is made, you can instantly meet different kinds of spirits. This is exactly how it is in the other world. To put it another way, in the other world, it is impossible to meet someone with whom you have no connection.

In the other world, if the spirits have no interest in one another, they cannot see each other even if they are in the same space. They each have their own spirit body and they are both the inhabitants of the other world, but they do not notice each other's presence. You might think they would crash into one another, but, actually, they walk through each other's bodies without realizing it.

If, on the other hand, a spirit is interested in another and wishes to speak or do something with it, one can see the other. Otherwise, they will pass by without noticing one another and it looks as if two ghosts are passing. This world on Earth actually coexists with this kind of Spirit World.

More than twenty years have passed since the foundation of Happy Science, and our elderly members will soon be reaching an age when they will begin returning to the other world. This means that it will be necessary to have spirits waiting to look after them when they arrive. We need people with knowledge of Buddha's Truth to return to the other world in order to guide those who follow. For this reason, several of my disciples have already made the journey back to the other world.

Returning to the other world is not something sad. If you have accomplished your tasks here on Earth, then there is nothing dreadful about the journey to the next world.

Spirits who bring news of their own death

I would now like to talk about spiritual experiences involving my relatives. This is the story of my grandmother on my father's side when she passed away.

She was the daughter of a monk and had been brought up in a temple in the Shikoku region of Japan. When she died, she had been living with her eldest son in Tokyo for two years. But before that, she had lived her entire life in Shikoku, so when she died, her spirit made its way back to her hometown.

My parents and aunt lived in Shikoku and, at exactly the time my grandmother died in Tokyo, the kitchen door opened about eight inches. It was a wooden, sliding door and everybody was surprised to see it slowly open by itself. It was only later that they learned this had occurred at the same time that my grandmother died.

This was the first spiritual experience I ever heard of, but looking into the matter later, I found that many such stories have been passed down, of people informing their relatives of their death in this way. There are large numbers of these sorts of reports.

This is particularly true of people who died during World War II. In many cases, their spirits returned to their hometowns from the battlefront in order to visit their parents and siblings. There are actually a lot of people who have experienced such spiritual phenomena.

The most common phenomenon was that the kitchen door slid open suddenly. In old times, the security of houses was not so tight, so it was probably quite easy for the doors to open. Other common experiences were hearing the voice of the dead person, hearing their footsteps, or hearing the sound of a spirit entering the room. There were also many physical phenomena, such as the bell on the family's Buddhist altar ringing suddenly in the middle of the night. The spirits make their presence known in these ways so that people can know someone is dead. There are many such reports.

It is also common for spirits to appear in dreams. The spirits of people who have died in war will most likely come to inform their relatives of their death. There have been many reports of such people appearing dressed as they were at the time of their death.

Monks living in temples often have spiritual experiences as well. It is said that monks are generally able to know in advance if there is going to be a funeral in the near future. They will wake in the night to hear the sound of footsteps in the main hall of the temple and then later somebody will come with news of a death nearby. This kind of experience is common.

When spirits cannot as a ghost directly inform people of their death, they may sometimes do it through animals. These kinds of occurrences have also been reported since ancient times. For instance, crows are quick to react to death and that is why people can guess that somebody has died when crows are upset.

Since the soul of the dead person is unable to communicate directly with the living, it possesses animals, causing them to make a commotion and inform others of their death. There are also cases in which domesticated animals or pets make a little commotion after the death of their owner. This is because the dead person's spirit is trying to communicate through these animals.

Another more unusual example is that of a black or yellow swallowtail butterfly flying into a house and then out again. In this case, the spirit of the dead person has temporarily possessed the butterfly in order to come back and tell others about its death.* So spirits sometimes do use animals or insects to transmit news of their own deaths. Such things really do happen.

Generally speaking, when a spirit comes, a door will open and the relatives will hear the sound of footsteps. In other cases, the bell on the family altar will chime. Sometimes the relatives can communicate with the spirit. In my grandmother's case, many of my relatives have talked of the door having slid open suddenly, so it must be a true story.

---

* For further examples, please refer to: Miyoko Matsutani, Chapter 3 of *Ikai-kara-no-Sain* [Signs from Another World](Chikuma Shobo Publishing); Shigeru Mizuki, Chapter 14 of *Kaikan-Ryoko* [Ghostly Travels](Chuko Bunko), etc.

A spirit's body is transparent
Several hours after death

Among my relatives was a man I will refer to as "T," who died some ten years ago. At that time, I knew that he was terminally ill and did not have much longer in this world.

The night he died, I was unable to sleep and got up around dawn to go to the bathroom. When I turned on the light, one of the two bulbs flickered and went out. "This is strange," I thought. I sensed that he was heading this way. I looked at the digital clock in the bathroom and saw the number "4:44." It was 4:44 in the morning, and the light bulb went out with a small pop.

It seems that spirits and electrical energy are related in some way and they are able to affect each other. The light bulb went out at 4:44 in the morning and I later heard that the person had died sometime around then.

"T" had died in Shikoku and I was living in Tokyo, yet at 11:30 that morning his spirit appeared in Tokyo, meaning that he had traveled several hundred miles in a matter of hours. When he came to me a few hours after his death, his body was transparent. I could see the kitchen crockery and cupboards clearly through his body. The vague form of his body could be seen as if it were made of gelatin or some other transparent material.

His facial features and outline were quite clear, but his legs seemed to wave around like seaweed growing out of the ocean floor and their shape was blurred. He had legs, but they wavered as if they were being seen through a heat haze. The rest of his body was visible but transparent.

I knew that he had died, but it was just prior to my giving a lecture at Tokyo Dome and I was unable to attend the funeral. So I recited to him the fundamental sutra of Happy Science, *Buddha's Teaching: The Dharma of the Right Mind*, and talked with him.

The funeral services that I hold are quite simple. If the spirit of a dead person comes to me, I recite our fundamental sutra and talk to them. I have a strong Dharma power, or spiritual power, to send spirits back to the other world so I do not need to conduct formal ceremonies.

This was one of my experiences. I learned at that time that spirits are able to travel hundreds of miles in a matter of hours after their death, that they have a transparent appearance, and that their legs are not clearly defined.

The spirit of a living company president Asking me for help

The spirits that come to visit me are not limited to those of the dead; sometimes even the spirits of the living appear before me. A soul is a complex entity, so it is possible for part of it to break away from the whole body in order to visit another person. I have met with such spirits of a living person a number of times.

When the Happy Science General Headquarters was still located in Kioicho, Chiyoda-ku, Tokyo, there was a president of a company who sometimes came to visit us at the office. I've heard that when he was very sick and had to have an operation, he listened avidly to the tapes of my lectures. Afterward he told me that the lectures saw him through his ordeal, so I think that he believed in Buddha's Truth. He was very interested in the Spirit World, but he retired from his company due to certain circumstances.

One summer when I was staying in the highland resort of Karuizawa where I had rented a log house, he became involved in a scandal. One day, I noticed a dark figure crouching in the corner of my room like a *ninja*. When I looked more closely, I realized that it was the spirit of the company president. The man was still alive, but his spirit had appeared before me, crouching down like a dark shadow. At that time, I did not know why he had come to see me, but I later read in the papers about the scandal he had been caught up in, and realized that he had been praying to me for help. His spirit was not transparent but dark, resembling someone's shadow.

In this way, a part of a living person's spirit body can appear in front of others. When a living person is in great danger, for example, their spirit can travel to appear in front of a person on whom they rely. This is a form of astral travel or out-of-body experience.

3

Various Phenomena Caused by a Soul Around the Time of Death

Souls that float in the air like death candles

What does it feel like to die? What happens to our spirit body when we die? If we look into books on this subject, we find they often describe how the soul experiences astral travel and that, in human form, the soul flies around the sky like Peter Pan. It can indeed feel this way to the dead person, but it does not necessarily mean that it actually appears like that externally.

In olden times, people often talked of "death candles" or "will-o'-the-wisps." It was said that when people died, they became a ball of fire, slightly larger than a man's fist, which burned with a bluish white or slightly orange light. When people saw one rising from the roof of a house, they would know that the inhabitant of the building would soon die. We often hear stories of a ball of fire rising out of the roof of the house of a terminally ill person shortly before he or she dies.

So when people die, the soul leaves the body, and although the person may believe that they are flying in human form, from the outside they actually appear like a ball of fire. It is difficult to see the exact moment that the soul leaves the body, but the soul has no hands or legs, and flies around as a ball of fire. This being the case, it is easy to understand how they can fly several hundred or even several thousand miles.

These death candles are generally visible through spiritual eyes, and I think that is why people living in the countryside or people in olden times were able to see them so often. It is also, however, possible for them to be seen through the physical senses.

In olden times, it was said that death candles were balls of flame. People have tried to explain them as phosphorus burning in the grave. There may be some who became interested enough to try and find out whether the flames are hot and, indeed, there have been people who have touched death candles. One reported that it felt like marshmallow or cotton candy, while another said it resembled the feel of silken fabric.

There was another inquisitive person who decided to investigate how much weight the body lost after dying and he came up with the answer of about 1.23 ounces and so concluded that a soul weighs 1.23 ounces. An ordinary set of household scales is generally only accurate to the nearest four to seven ounces, so I am not sure how he arrived at this figure, but it is said that the body becomes lighter after death. Speaking from experience, I can say that the body does appear to get lighter after death. I have not personally weighed a body before and after death, so I do not know exactly, but it is reported like that.*

Nonetheless, people take on the form of a ball of flame when they leave the body. In ancient India, the soul was said to be about the size of a man's thumb and it would leave when the body died. It was considered to be a kind of substance, be it small or large. It seems to be true to say that something leaves the body after death.

A tale of a man who caught
A death candle in a basin

It was once reported in Iwate Prefecture, in northern Japan, that somebody captured a death candle. He was a man who worked in the local prefectural office.

One night he was in his house and, glancing toward the entrance, suddenly saw a death candle. He realized immediately what it was and, grabbing a broom, chased it around the hall until he was finally able to capture it under an overturned basin. It sounds like a scene out of the movie *Ghostbusters*, but he succeeded in capturing a death candle with a basin.

---

* For further information, refer to Miyoko Matsutani, *Gendai Minwa-ko V* [Thoughts on Contemporary Folk Tales V] [Rippu Shobo Publishing]; also *Gendai Minwa-ko 5* [Chikuma Bunko].

A short while later, one of his neighbors came and said, "You have to come quickly; your uncle has just died!" His uncle lived quite close. He had been confined to his bed for a long time and everybody knew the end was near. When the nephew heard the news, he thought that he had better go and pay his last respects.

As he was about to leave, his thoughts turned to the death candle he had trapped. "I suppose I had better let it go," he thought and, lifting the basin, allowed it to escape. He walked to his uncle's house, arriving to find that the dead man had suddenly opened his eyes and begun to breathe again. "How dare you chase your uncle around like that?" the older man reprimanded his nephew. "I cannot believe you trapped me in a basin." The man had actually caught his uncle's soul and, with the soul unable to return to the body, the uncle had died.

When death is approaching after a long illness, it is not unusual for the soul to slip in and out of the body. In the case of the uncle, when his soul left the body, it became trapped, and with the soul unable to return, he was confirmed as dead. Once the soul was released and able to return, however, the man came back to life, cursing his nephew for capturing him. Of course, the nephew had not known that the death candle had been his uncle's soul and he shuddered with horror.

This is an example of a man capturing his uncle's soul, and it was confirmed that the uncle came back to life. Most likely, the uncle did not realize that he was flying in the form of a death candle; he probably believed that he had walked to his nephew's house in human form, and that was why he was so angry about having been chased with a broom and trapped. Such incidents have actually been recorded and are so graphic that I believe they are accounts of true events.*

So the soul sometimes leaves the body temporarily before death and it is possible to see a death candle several days before death actually occurs. This indicates that the soul has begun practicing for its departure to the other world. That is why it is difficult to confirm the exact moment of death.

A tale of a woman who came back to life To kill her husband's mistress

There are also numerous tales from western Japan of people who came back to life. One example involved

---

*Refer to Miyoko Matsutani, *Gendai Minwa-ko IV* [Thoughts on Contemporary Folk Tales IV](Rippu Shobo Publishing); *Gendai Minwa-ko 4* (Chikuma Bunko); Kunio Yanagita, *Tono-Monogatari, Fu, Tono-Monogatari-Shui 151* [Tales of Tono, Supplement 151] (Kadokawa Bunko), etc.

a wealthy man in Osaka who owned a large house. He lived in this house with his wife and his mistress. Naturally, the wife and mistress despised each other, but they pretended to get along for appearance's sake.

Eventually, the wife fell sick and died before the mistress. A wake was held and those who attended retired to separate rooms for the night. In the middle of the night, eerie noises were heard in the corridor, like a stick striking the floor. The sounds were terrifying. The house was an ancient one and a spear was displayed on a rack. The dead wife actually came back to life, took down the spear, and made her way to the mistress's room, using the spear as a walking stick. Then she opened the door, killed the mistress with the spear, and fell down dead once again.*

This is a story that exists on record. It shows the dreadful hatred that gripped the wife, making her determined to take her husband's mistress with her. If she retained these sorts of feelings, she could have become a demon in the next world, so she may have had no other choice but to let go of her resentment in this way. In fact, it is quite common for people with powerful obsessions to return to life even after they have died.

---

* Refer to Miyoko Matsutani, *Gendai-Minwa-ko V* [Thoughts on Contemporary Folk Tales V].

There is also a story recorded in northeast Japan in which an old woman lying in a coffin got up in the middle of the night and walked past the hearth. As she passed, a round charcoal container turned slightly, showing that she had touched it physically.*

From what I have described here, you can see that, shortly before and after death, the soul can cause different kinds of phenomena. If you have some attachment to this world, you cannot return to the other world immediately.

The more we hear this kind of story, the more we can realize the importance of the ancient Buddhist teaching, "Do not hold on to attachments." Buddhism teaches that people who retain attachments to this world will not be able to return to the other world, so we must work to abandon any attachments.

This teaching is indeed right, and it is particularly important for people in their old age. Once they realize they are not long for this world, they should work to tidy their affairs so they will leave no problems behind when they die.

Sometimes death can be foreseen, but sometimes it comes all of a sudden. When a person knows how much life remains to them, they will be able to make

---

* Matsutani, op. cit.; Kunio Yanagita, Chapter 22 of *Tono-Monogatari* [Tales of Tono](Kadokawa Bunko), etc.

the necessary preparations and will not have strong attachments, but there are people who die much earlier than expected as a result of illness or accident. In such cases, if they have not solved their worldly problems, they will find it difficult to return to Heaven.

As you grow older, you must clear up all matters that are troubling you, one by one. Of course, people sometimes die suddenly in their forties or fifties, so you should always try to settle your problems in case of some unexpected happening. By doing so, you will find that there will be fewer impediments to your journey into the next life.

I am sure that people who have studied for a long time at Happy Science do not have many attachments, but if they have not made sufficient preparations, they may find themselves in the same situation.

Spirits wish to communicate their thoughts
To people in this world

One of the hardest things for spirits who have returned to the next world is that they are unable to communicate with people who are still alive. From their viewpoint, it is very inconvenient. Some spirits may think, "There is one thing I forgot to say before I died and I did not put it in my will either." Since few people are capable of hearing the voices of spirits, this is very hard on them.

Speaking from my own plentiful experience, however, I believe that it is a good thing that ordinary people cannot see or hear spirits. If people could see spirits or hear their voices, they would not be able to live peacefully.

As I mentioned earlier, I am protected by a spiritual screen that keeps out all spirits except for a certain few or those from the higher realms. One day, however, when I was lying in bed, thinking about giving a lecture on life after death, I was approached by all kinds of spiritual beings, asking me to talk about them. It was a very busy night.

Perhaps I was sending out the thought that I intended to talk about life after death and having done so, many spirits expected that I would include the stories of dead people. So they all came to ask me to tell their stories. All these spirits who are generally unable to reach me appeared at about twelve midnight, and they continued gossiping until two or three in the morning. Some spirits even asked me, "Will you mention my name?" "There is something I wanted to say before I died so could you pass it on for me?" In this way, the entire night was interrupted by the voices of spirits.

They are not always spirits who failed to return to Heaven. Among spirits who have already returned to the next world, there are some who wish to send messages to those who are still alive, because they are unable to communicate with the living. This is like passing on their greetings after having changed their address.

I spoke earlier of the actor, K. N. He had entered Heaven smoothly so there was no problem, but the day after his death, he came to me and asked if I would look after his wife and daughter for him, saying that they were his only worry. I told him that they were financially stable so there was nothing for him to worry about. "I know, and I'm very grateful," he replied, "but please make sure they are all right." This was the only worry he had and as it was his last wish, I felt an obligation. So I was more or less attentive to their needs.

He knew that his messages would be heard if he came to me, so I listened to what he had to say. I won't deal with all the other minor requests, but I do my best to carry out the wishes that are most important to a spirit.

The writer T. K. also returned to Heaven sometime after he died. Later, as he became accustomed to his good life in Heaven, he came to visit me and asked if I would publish a book of his spiritual messages. I told him that I usually do not publish the spiritual messages of people who have only recently returned to Heaven because they haven't reached the rank of god.

In truth, a message from a newly returned spirit does not have much value. Unless they have lived in the Spirit World for several hundred years, they will be disregarded for being too human. Such spirits do not have sufficient status to give spiritual messages. I also told him that I was not eager to publish the spiritual messages of my disciples. I have my position and cannot favor a particular disciple. As a result, he agreed to limit his message to a short handwritten note.

This kind of discussion with the dead sometimes occurs. Not all dead people have attachments or obsessive desires, but many of them feel that they were unable to say a sufficient farewell to the people they left behind. So if they have the opportunity, they are eager to say a proper goodbye. That is why they sometimes come back to this world as a ghost and, as I described earlier, make all kinds of spiritual phenomena happen.

4

Entering the Spirit World and Going to Heaven or Hell

Spirits will first reflect on their life on Earth

Spirits of dead people must leave this world in about forty-nine days after they die. Actually, there is a general rule that they should not remain wandering on Earth for more than about three weeks after their death. At the very longest, they must leave after about forty-nine days. In less than two months, they will be told that it's time to leave and they must let go of this world.

Up until that time, they are left to do as they like. They are not yet ready to enter the other world completely, so they travel back and forth between this world and the next. They wander around and watch people in this world. They are concerned about how their funeral is proceeding, how their property is being passed on, how their company is being managed, whether their children are in harmony with one another, or whether their spouse is seeing someone else. So they linger in this world for almost two months. After this period, however, they are told that it's time to leave.

Actually, when people die, a spirit or guide comes and takes them to the next world, but they tend to return to this world once again. They are permitted to stay here for a while so they can study the differences between the next world and this one. As time passes, they become accustomed to being a spirit and their physical or materialistic attributes gradually drop away. Around this time, it is suggested to them that they leave this world and enter the next.

Eventually, they will come to the River Styx and, once they have passed over this river, they will truly become dead to this world. Then they arrive at the entrance to the Spirit World, or what is referred to as the Astral or Posthumous Realm.

On the opposite bank of the River Styx, they usually see a vast field full of rape blossoms and other beautiful flowers and they will find deceased relatives, their friends, and various other people welcoming them. Many people believe that they have arrived in Heaven. This is not exactly Heaven, however; it is the Astral Realm. The Astral Realm is a place where people first go after death and wait until it is determined whether they will go to Heaven or Hell.

In the same way that people remain in this world for some time after death, they also spend a while in that realm and live as a spirit, reflecting on their lives before their final destination is decided. During this period, they are shown their whole life in the form of a movie, or a guiding spirit may come to discuss various events that happened in their life, one at a time.

Since we have movies on Earth today, in the next world people's lives are often presented as a kind of movie. Sometimes a person's life is displayed in a kind of mirror. In the old days, when people did not yet know of screen images, it is said that they were presented with a notebook in which all the deeds of their life on Earth were listed. In Buddhist and Hindu countries, this notebook is called the "Records of Yama," *Yama* being the supreme judge of Hell.

The scientist, philosopher, and mystic Emanuel Swedenborg [1688-1772], who left a vast amount of written material on the Spirit World in his *Experiences in the Afterworld*, reports having seen the following:

"One spirit was called for its turn to repent the deeds he carried out in life. When he was on earth, this man had received bribes and done illegal transactions, all of which he kept a close record of in a little notebook. As the judge spirit stared at his face and his entire body, the notebook he had written suddenly came out of the ground and, at his feet, the pages fluttered open allowing all the other spirits there to see what he had done.

"This notebook even contained records of things that the man had forgotten he had done. It listed everything that the man had thought and done while he was alive on earth, and as the pages turned, the other spirits were able to see his thoughts and deeds. What is more, there were even things that he had never written. He was so surprised and shocked."

In olden times, this was the way people saw the details of their lives. When they reflected on their past thoughts and deeds, sometimes these records appeared in written form. But today it is much more common for people's lives to be presented in the form of a movie or as images in a mirror. So, after having, in the Astral Realm, reflected on their life, their destination in the next world will finally be decided.

The reason why the other world separated into Heaven and Hell

Today, Heaven and Hell are clearly separated, but this has not always been the case. As the population of Hell increased, it became necessary to separate its inhabitants, leading to a clear division. Far in the past, however, there was a time when Heaven and Hell coexisted in a world similar to the Astral Realm.

At that time, the heaven-oriented spirits lived on a hill. In this world on Earth, when you purchase a house, you will often find a site with a nice view is more expensive than one that has no view. In the same way, spirits who had a heavenly consciousness liked to live on a hill. On the other hand, spirits who are now classified as hellish spirits or lower-level spirits lived around the bottom of the hill, among the ponds, marshes, and caves. Some lived underground in damp, marshy areas.

You may find it strange that a heavenly place like the Astral Realm and a hellish place would coexist in the fourth dimension, and completely different beings would live together in the same dimension. But this is how it was originally. Heaven-oriented spirits would live in a place with a nice view while hell-oriented spirits lived in the marshes and caves. This situation lasted for a long time.

Since both types of spirits lived in the same neighborhood, however, they often came into contact with each other, which frequently resulted in leaving both parties with unpleasant feelings. They would both find the experience disagreeable and the more they met, the more they disliked each other. So as time passed, they gradually kept a greater distance between them.

As more spirits wished that the hell-oriented spirits would go away, the latter were forced further underground and their dwelling place grew until it became a great underworld kingdom. The heavenly spirits thought, "We don't like to be with them, so we wish our world would become more fitting for us." That is how the Spirit World was clearly divided in two.

The other world is a world of thought. So if everybody discusses and decides what kind of town they would like to create, what kind of living environment they want, and unites their thoughts, then the town will take on that appearance.

The spirits who lived around the ponds and marshes or in the caves are like the homeless that roam our cities today. They were similar to the seedy tramps that we sometimes come across living in parks. So other spirits said, "If we don't isolate them, the value of our town will decrease. We don't want them around so let's keep them away." Then large numbers of spirits combined their willpower to drive them underground and put up a barrier, separating them from the rest of the realm. This is how a new realm was created underground and it gradually expanded. This was why Heaven and Hell first separated and Hell grew much larger.

Today, those who have achieved a certain level of enlightenment on Earth are able to return straight to Heaven after they die, whereas others drop straight to Hell. Otherwise, it is often said that the journey to the next world resembles passing through a tunnel. In the past, I have talked about this myself. Many people who have undergone near-death experiences have described it as traveling through a dark tunnel until they emerge suddenly in a brilliant world.

However, this tunnel that leads to the light, the tunnel between dimensions, sometimes opens downward.

People who experience this will first find themselves in a strange world they do not understand. Wandering around, they will come across a large hole in the ground that resembles a well or a manhole. "I wonder what this is," they might say, as they look into it, and then find themselves sucked into it, traveling downward as if they were on an elevator and reaching their designated realm in Hell.

So there is a dark tunnel that heads downward, leading you to Hell. It feels very much as if you are falling down toward the center of the Earth. This is another form of a hole between dimensions. There are not many examples of this kind of experience, but it has been reported like this.

Originally, there was no clear division between Heaven and Hell; the only division between the two areas existed on a horizontal plane. This is similar to Manhattan in New York City, with dangerous slum areas, where even a police car will be completely stripped if left unattended, existing side-by-side with wealthy areas. This is how it was with Heaven and Hell, the two being divided on a horizontal plane.

The inhabitants could not stand this situation indefinitely, however, and were gradually separated into different dimensions. A large number of inhabitants shared the same image of their world and gradually changed their world to fit this vision. That is the way things work in the other world.

You can study this kind of world and also the higher realms at Happy Science; I have taught a lot about higher realms. But the majority of people have different kinds of spiritual experiences of the not-so-high realms of the Spirit World.

The light of the Spiritual Sun does not reach Hell

Earlier, I stated that Hell had its origins in caves or in the damp, boggy land around marshes and ponds, but it does not mean that physically there are rocks and caves. They are not real matter but merely a form of thought energy. What makes them appear is the preference for dark, damp, and dank places, or the feeling of wanting to hide from the light. Light reveals evil, so the inhabitants wish to avoid the light. This feeling of wanting to avoid the light will invite similar thought energy, thus creating Hell.

The light of the Spiritual Sun does not reach Hell. But there are also places where a dull red glow, similar to that of a sunset, reaches. The spirits of Hell live in a realm that is very close to this world and the Spiritual Sun can sometimes be seen shining dimly in the blackness of their sky. You would think that it was the moon, but it is, in fact, the Spiritual Sun.

If the spirits in Hell are exposed to the light of the Spiritual Sun, they find it too bright and, to be more exact, it is painful for them. In this respect, they are very much like moles. Moles are able to tell the difference between light and dark, but they are virtually blind and live their entire lives underground. It is said that moles are unable to live for a long time aboveground. In the same way, the spirits of Hell prefer living underground because their minds have a tendency to avoid the light.

You may think that they would be happy if somebody provided them with light, but this is not the case. They are like cockroaches, spiders, or rats. They are not pleased when a light comes on in the night and they scuttle out of sight. Only when it is dark do they come out and, in the same way, the lost souls of Hell dislike the light. They hate being exposed to the light of the Spiritual Sun and cannot live unless they have surrounded themselves with things to obstruct the light. That is why the light of the Spiritual Sun is weakened in Hell.

Worldly desires are the force
That sustains life in Hell

The main power that sustains life in Hell is worldly desires. All human beings on Earth have worldly desires to some degree. These are, for example, selfish desires, the desire for self-preservation, me-ism [which is always saying, "Me, me!" or "I am the most important!" or "I want to do this!"], and the desire for material objects and for money. These are actually part of the desire to live, but these desires serve as the source of energy that sustains life in Hell.

There are people who have grown old and are nearing death but who still have lots of desires and say, "I want more and more!" They are the ones who must watch out. As you grow old, your body will become infirm, your legs will become incapable of bearing your weight, and you may be confined to a wheelchair or bed. At this time, you should start letting go of your worldly desires and gradually forget them. When you grow old, you must start to think more about the next world than about this one. That is why your faculties will begin to fail, so that you will want to move on to the next world.

Despite this, if your greed simply becomes stronger and you exert yourself even more, you will find this energy being converted into the energy of Hell. So you must be careful.

Even the beings living in Hell sometimes run out of energy, so they come out to tap into the energy of living people. Spirits of Hell come to steal the energy of people on Earth. They search for the energy of people that is of a similar nature to their own. In the same way that a car will not run properly without the right fuel, these spirits come to look for energy of the same nature as their own. In this way, they take the energy they need to fuel their desires and are unable to live without that kind of power.

Generally speaking, spirits of Hell are all selfish. They are selfish, self-centered, and think of nothing but themselves. When forming personal relationships, they only think about whether the person will benefit them, serve them, or be of use to them. This is all they think of and they do not want relationships other than those with people who can be their servants or prey.

On the other hand, the majority of spirits in Heaven wish to be of service to others. Being the kind of spirits they are, they are able to live together, but they cannot coexist peacefully with those who have the minds of vagabonds. As a result, both groups chose to live separately from one another. In a way, they both prefer it like that.

Hell is indeed a place of torment, so the spirits in Hell desperately try to escape from there. To relieve their suffering, they spend as much time as possible possessing people on Earth. They also try to increase their numbers in order to take their mind off their pain and attempt to make people on Earth live the same way they did.

For instance, if a person destroyed his life on Earth as a result of an alcohol addiction, after dying, he will possess another alcoholic or somebody with tendencies toward alcoholism, making him or her drink ever more, thereby destroying that person's life.

The same is true of those who were addicted to gambling. A person who fell deep into debt and went bankrupt as a result of betting on horses or bicycle racing, and who led his whole family to commit suicide, will come back to the racetracks after death. As he comes across somebody else who likes gambling, he possesses that person and causes him or her to walk the same road to ruin. He will take pleasure in doing such things.

I am sure that all of you are able to understand the feeling of pleasure at seeing others' happiness being destroyed when you cannot find happiness for yourself. There are people who give up on achieving happiness themselves, and instead find happiness in repeatedly trying to make others unhappy to relieve their own misery.

5

Understanding the Meaning of Soul Training on Earth

It is impossible to prevent suicide
Without knowing the truth about the Spirit World

There are people who do not realize that they are a spiritual being, a soul, even after they have died. I suppose that there are people who commit suicide, thinking that life will become easier in the other world if they die. The vast majority of those who commit suicide, however, do not believe in the next world.

They think, "This world is full of pain, but life ends in this world. So if I die, my debts will disappear, the pain I experience in personal relationships will disappear, the pain of being fired from my job will disappear. If I die, then all my problems will be solved." They then jump off a building or commit suicide in another way, but it takes these spirits a long time to realize their existence as souls.

As a result, even after they have arrived in the next world, they continue to commit suicide by jumping off tall buildings. When they do this, their bodies are smashed by the impact with the ground and blood flows from their wounds. It has the same effect as when they jumped in this world; their bodies are destroyed and there is blood everywhere. "This time I have managed to die," they think, but after a short while, their bodies repair themselves and they return to their original state. They then stand up, climb to the top of the building, and jump off again, repeating this many times.

After a while, they tire of this endless repetition and return to the building in this world where they originally committed suicide. They search for someone who looks as though he wishes to die, then possess him, and they jump together.

There are many cliffs by the sea that are famous for the number of suicides that happen there. The numbers are so high because the spirits of those who have previously committed suicide drag other people to their deaths. They look for someone who is wandering around, deep in worry, then possess him and make him feel that the spirit's emotions are his own, and make him commit suicide. In this way, they continue to increase their numbers until a specific spiritual field is created in that place, which becomes like a kind of Hell. So Hell is created in places that are famous as sites for suicides.

Not knowing the truth is indeed frightening. There are people who commit suicide without knowing that there is life after death and there are others who do so while believing that they will go to Heaven. Unfortunately, however, both remain unable to enter Heaven.

Even though you die on Earth, life continues in the next world. Your life is eternal, so if you want to return to Heaven after you die, while you are still on Earth you must live with a mind that is in accordance with that of the inhabitants of Heaven. This is the requirement for returning to Heaven.

If you want to know whether you will go to Heaven or not, think about whether you have the same state of mind as the inhabitants of Heaven. Do you think it is possible for people who have been driven into a corner and who die in anguish to return to Heaven? Ask yourself this and you will know the answer for yourself.

In Japan, more than thirty thousand people a year choose to commit suicide. It is a terrible thing and of these people, approximately twenty thousand are middle aged or seniors. It is said that twenty thousand middle-aged and elderly people choose to commit suicide because they have come to a dead end in their work. There is an urgent need to stop these suicides, but without knowledge of the truth about the Spirit World, it is impossible to find a countermeasure to deal with this problem.

What we must tell people who are thinking about committing suicide is just to put aside their pride and vanity because the only thing they can take back with them to the other world when they die is their own mind.

Today, there is very little possibility of people in Japan starving to death; even the homeless people living in parks are suffering from diabetes. No matter how hard their financial situation, no matter how their reputation or pride may be destroyed, it is always possible to make a fresh start. If you believe that life is limited to this world, then you will feel your future is hopeless and you may well want to die. Once you know that life continues beyond death, however, you will certainly not commit suicide.

People who suffer in this world will find that, after they have died, their suffering is increased tenfold or even a hundredfold. Conversely, those who savored heavenly joy while living in this world will experience ten times, one hundred times as much joy after they return to the next world. Our thoughts in this world will be amplified in the next.

If you go to a world of pain after death, you will find that the pain you suffered in this world will be amplified until pain is all that seems to exist. While you are living on Earth, you may suffer pain for some of the time, but there must be other times when you experience other emotions. In the world of pain that exists in the next world, however, there is nothing but pain, all the time. Therefore suicide is not worth all the suffering you will experience later.

When you were born into this world, you brought

nothing with you. You were born naked as a baby and have lived some decades since then. If you accept the premise that when you die, you can take only your mind, then you will know that you should abandon your attachments and reflect on your past thoughts and deeds. While it may be impossible for you to rebuild your life completely, you can try to fix it as much as possible before you return to the next world.

This world is a physical one and the soul training you carry out here is extremely hard, but it is about ten times more effective than the training done in the next word. Therefore, if you spend a whole year in this world practicing self-reflection, you will find that it is the equivalent of ten years' worth in the next world.

The source of suffering in this world is mostly egoistic desire, a worldview centered on oneself and on the values of this world. In other words, suffering arises from a worldview that focuses only on this world and yourself. Some people may end up making others suffer or shortening their own lives because they find it too difficult to live through their own lives. But they must change their way of thinking.

What I have talked about here is the simple and most basic teaching from the standpoint of somebody who has a deep understanding of Buddha's Truth. At the very least, I would like the majority of people around the world to know this basic truth.

You can be an angel or a devil
Through your thoughts

In addition to that, I would like you to know that angels are not merely imaginary creatures that appear in old stories. They are not specific beings that God created in ancient times. Angels are spirits who continuously try to save and bring happiness to as many people as possible through their reincarnations and who work to lead others in the next world as well. This is a fact that you need to know.

Angels were formerly human beings; they have experienced life as people. Human history is much longer than is generally known and all the beings that have been described as angels or gods over the last few thousand years originally lived here on Earth as human beings. They guided large numbers of people while they were on Earth and continued their work in the next world. I want you to know that it is possible for you, too, to become an angel or, alternatively, a devil.

Angels and devils were not created as such; they become what they are as a result of the manifestation of their own thoughts. People who are always angry and have frightening expressions on their faces may look like demons. They almost look as if they have horns, wide mouths, and huge fangs, and when they return to the other world, this form will manifest itself. If in their heart they think like a demon, then they will naturally take on that appearance.

On the other hand, if you have the heart of an angel, then you will appear as an angel in the next world. You need to know that souls usually recognize themselves as having a human form, but essentially they have total freedom to change their shape and appearance.

Reconsidering the nobility of humankind

People who do not appreciate their life as a human being will find that, after death, they have fallen to the Hell of Beasts, one of the realms in Hell, where they will live their lives in animal form. If they still do not learn their lesson, their soul may reincarnate in an animal's body to undergo soul training on Earth for a certain period of time. This is something that really does happen.

Please imagine how it would feel to live on Earth for several years in a form other than human, be it as a cow, a pig, a horse, or a cat. You may now lead your life grumbling and complaining, saying only bad things about others, holding grudges against your parents, society, or the company you are working for, resenting that you cannot get promoted, that you have little money or cannot get enough to eat. But please think about what it would be like if you lived as a stray cat for two years. How would you see humans through your cat eyes?

Then you would understand that human beings appear like kings and queens; their lives would seem so free and affluent that they would all seem to be royalty. You would come to realize how fortunate you are to be a human being.

There are some who have to undertake such extreme training before they can understand human dignity. There are indeed these kinds of people. The spirit body can transform itself freely, so it is actually possible for it to take the form of any creature. Having said this, however, there is a general rule that human spirits usually reincarnate as humans.

I hope that, on this occasion, you will reconsider the nobility of humankind, and realize the meaning of your soul training here on Earth. Please understand how important it is to live on the basis of the knowledge that life after death really does exist.

Chapter Two

The Principle of Spiritual Possession

~ How to Protect Yourself from Evil Spirits ~

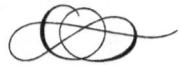

Lecture given on February 11, 2004

1
Modern Science Cannot Explain The Phenomenon of Possession

In the past people understood the word possession

The subject of this chapter is "The Principle of Spiritual Possession." I have talked about the principle of possession on numerous occasions, but I have never treated it as a main theme. Since Happy Science often talks about spiritual possession as a matter of fact, I would like to take this opportunity to explain its meaning and the mechanism in detail.

The Japanese characters that make up the word *possession* are quite difficult and I presume there are not many Japanese people today who can read or write it. These characters are not taught at school and the only people who know them are those who have studied Japanese literature or religion. I think that for anybody else, these characters are too difficult to read or write.

In the past, the word *possession* was well known. Up until World War II, many people would talk about spiritual possession and this idea was commonly accepted. People who were educated in the postwar period, however, might well have never even heard of the word. Today, people who talk about spiritual possession are thought to be rather strange.

Western medicine treats possession As a malfunction of the brain

If we exclude religion, the only field that deals with possession is medicine or, more precisely, psychiatry. Therefore, if people claim that they are spiritually possessed, that they see or hear spirits, they will most likely be sent to a psychiatrist. Spiritual possession is something that indeed requires some psychological help, so this tendency cannot be completely denied.

At its present level, however, contemporary medicine is unable to explain the phenomenon of possession scientifically. Western medicine seems to know about this phenomenon, but cannot say why it occurs and is unable to explain it scientifically or medically.

Medicine is a science based on the study of the physical body, so at its root is a materialistic way of thinking. Medical science certainly has a role in society, but when confronted with the phenomenon of possession, doctors can only search for a physical cause and they tend to treat it as a problem related to the workings or the structure of the brain. When looked at from a psychiatric viewpoint, possession is generally put down to some kind of malfunction of the brain.

Furthermore, doctors believe that people's feelings arise together with the workings of the brain. They think that since the mind is simply a function of the brain, a person's mental condition depends purely on the condition of the brain; if something is wrong with the brain, then the workings of a person's mind will also be distorted. That is why if somebody says that they can see or hear spirits, and if they claim that they are the spirit of some famous person, they are treated as psychiatric patients.

Many people are sent to psychiatric hospitals for this reason, but fundamentally, these hospitals are unable to cure people of spiritual possession. They have no way of curing it because medical science does not understand the phenomenon of possession. All they are able to do is medicate the person, keep them quiet, and lock them away in an institution to avoid friction with the general public.

When a spiritual phenomenon like this occurs, if there is nobody close to the victim who understands the spiritual truth, the poor person is likely to be locked away in a mental institution. I feel very sorry for these kinds of people.

In the past, such matters were dealt with in temples. In those days, there were many priests or monks who had Dharma power. Many Buddhist monks and Shinto priests, as well as other religious practitioners, had acquired a kind of psychic power accumulated through spiritual training. So in the past when spiritual phenomena occurred, people would say, "He has been possessed by an evil spirit," or "She has been possessed by a fox or raccoon," and would take the person to a priest to have the spirit exorcised.

Today, however, all religious or spiritual matters have been completely cut out of the general education system. They have been removed and are never mentioned. By ignoring spirituality in this way, the schools are, in effect, denying such phenomena. As a result, people today have nowhere to learn spiritual knowledge and they do not even think of the possibility that somebody might be possessed. They have no way of making any judgments and, consequently, they send the possessed person to a hospital, when, in fact, they should consult a psychic. Then, having no idea what is causing the problem, the hospital simply writes it off as a disease of the brain and keeps the person in an institution.

Of course, some people may become mentally disturbed because of actual damage to the brain, so, in some cases, the problem lies in the body itself. However, there are many cases where the cause is a spiritual one and the problem lies in the mind. Because there is some problem in the person's mind, they can see or hear spirits.

Having said this, however, although claims such as "Many spirits are visiting me" or "Somebody's spirit is here now" sound strange to the modern ear, in reality, these claims are completely true from the viewpoint of the Real World.*

* In his *Genshisuru-Kindai-Kukan* [Modern Space in Hallucinations](Seikyusha Publishing), Kunimitsu Kawamura explains how after the westernization of Japan in the mid-nineteenth century, spiritual phenomena came to be treated as mere superstition and were thought to be a result of mental or neurological functions.

2

Possession Means to Be Haunted By a Spirit

Humans are spiritual beings

This three-dimensional world where we live appears to be a vast and boundless place, but it only appears large because we are now living in it. From the perspective of the vast Spirit World, this world is like a tiny space that floats in the Spirit World. The Spirit World itself is extremely large.

While it is possible to measure the circumference and diameter of planet Earth, the Spirit World is so immense that it is impossible to measure or even estimate its size. No one knows its total size. In one part of this vast Spirit World, there is a field related to physical objects, and that is the three-dimensional world where humans are living. This is the truth and, unless you change your way of thinking, you will not be able to understand any of the spiritual truths.

As I have taught repeatedly in the past, humans are spiritual beings, and their spiritual existence is their true self. Humans spend long years living as spiritual beings and their real life belongs to the Spirit World. While living in the Spirit World, however, the material world undergoes various developments. Therefore, when a new age arises, spirits come down to live for a time on Earth to create new relationships with people, enjoy the changes in the physical environment, and gain new experiences. Having gained new enlightenment and a new personality, they eventually return to the Spirit World.

After returning to the Spirit World, they live on the fourth, fifth, or sixth dimension for a time in the same form as they took on Earth, but in time their experiences of life on Earth become outdated. They are then unable to understand what the new returnees are talking about and find them looking very different.

Spirits in the other world work as a guardian spirit, guiding spirit, or supporting spirit, helping people living on Earth, but gradually they find themselves unable to understand what is happening on Earth. When this happens, they decide to set out once more and are born on Earth where they learn new ways or a new sense of life. Humans repeatedly reincarnate on Earth in this way.

Seen from the Spirit World, This world is a precarious place

The Spirit World and this world are related to one another, but what is valued in this world differs greatly from what is valued in the Spirit World; the values are usually completely reversed. In fact, life in the Spirit World is the true life, or the main life of the soul. People on Earth are blind to this spiritual life, however, and they are living using only about 10 percent of their true senses.

From the viewpoint of the Spirit World or the spirit body, life on Earth is like a trip down the shaft of an excavated coal mine, which is several hundred or several thousand feet deep, with only the light on your helmet. That is how precarious this world appears from the Spirit World. Although you have a light, you are surrounded by darkness and you cannot really tell where you are walking.

People in this world believe that their eyes are open and they can see everything. But seen from the other world, people living in this world are blind. People on Earth are only able to see the three-dimensional world, so from the standpoint of the Real World, their eyes see nothing.

It is said that a large number of animals and insects are incapable of seeing color; they see everything in black and white. From the viewpoint of the other world, people on Earth are no different. They are only capable of seeing things vaguely in black and white, like the images on an old television or in old photographs. They are incapable of seeing the truth and they appear rather vulnerable.

To the eyes of the guardian and guiding spirits in the other world, life on Earth is akin to traveling several thousand feet down a pitch-black tunnel with only one small light to see by. So these spirits are always worrying about you because this world appears dangerous and accidents are inclined to happen. They stand at the mouth of this long tunnel and shout out to you, "Hey, are you alright? The exit is this way!" They are able to talk to us in this way, but it is difficult for people on Earth to find their way without getting lost.

This is how life on Earth is. Unless you are able to look at it from the perspective of the Spirit World, you cannot see the real state of this world. The material world exists under a set of such extraordinarily special conditions.

In order to live in this world, where one must rely on food and other material objects, humans are provided with physical bodies. Like other animals, these bodies come with an instinct to live. If people follow their instincts, they will be able to survive. If they eat when they are hungry and do as their body demands, they are generally able to live. Humans are given instincts like a screw propeller for living through life in this world. While people are living on Earth, however, they tend to forget about the Spirit World.

Some people may ask why we forget about the Spirit World. People who do not believe in the Spirit World, such as some scientists, might ask, "Why do we lose the memories of the Spirit World? Why should we forget it? It is very strange that this should happen." However, what would happen if we were able to see, hear, and feel spirits? Life here in the third dimension would become much more difficult.

Spirits can overlay each other

There are completely different principles in the other world. For instance, in this world, if you try to place two fists in the same place, they will strike each other. Each of the fists has a separate existence, so they cannot both be present in the same space. That is one of the laws of this world. In this world, it is impossible for two objects to exist in the same space. If there are different objects, they will strike each other. That is the relationship they share.

On the other hand, the laws of the Spirit World differ and it is possible for two objects to occupy the same space. This means that if two spirits walk into each other, even if their bodies come into contact, they can pass through each other's bodies. If they are aware of each other, they will recognize when they pass through each other, but if their consciousness is focused on something else, they can pass through each other without even realizing it. This is quite a common occurrence.

In this world it is impossible to pass through a wall, but spirits have no trouble walking through walls. In the Spirit World, different entities can exist in the same place simultaneously and are capable of passing through each other.

The principle of possession is related to this. While it is physically impossible for two objects to exist in the same place, when it comes to spirits, two or three can overlie one another.

In a human's body resides a spirit body, which is slightly larger than the physical body. These two bodies make up a human on Earth. But what would happen if another spirit were to enter the physical body? Of course, spirits can physically ride on something or they can push someone from behind, but they can also overlap other spirits. This is how a spirit can coexist in the same body of a person.

Possession is a state
In which a spirit affects a person on Earth

Academically, the word *possession* refers mainly to a phenomenon that is visible to the human eye. I am sure that you have heard of shamans who live in jungles in tropical or subtropical regions. They are holy people who hold séances, go into trances, and take on a different personality. They dance, sing, and suddenly break into speech, and their communion with the Spirit World sometimes lasts for up to an hour or two.

During this time, the spirit of an ancestor may enter a shaman's body or one of the gods may speak through the shaman, putting him or her into an unnatural state. Onlookers can tell right away that the shaman is acting in an unusual manner. When the spirit expresses itself violently though a person's body in a way that is visible to others, it is often called the "phenomenon of possession" in the fieldwork.

Since ancient times, similar phenomena have been witnessed in Japan. When Shinto priests or priestesses wave a staff decorated with strips of paper and call the gods down upon them, spirits come down to possess their bodies, shaking it uncontrollably.

Another example can be seen in voodoo, often criticized as a pagan religion. This religion, with its roots in Africa, is popular in Haiti and has become the dominant faith in that area. Voodoo also invites spirits into its believers and, during festivals, large numbers of people are possessed, their bodies controlled by outside forces.

This phenomenon can be commonly observed in regions where religions have been passed down from ancient times, places such as Africa, Indonesia, and South America, among others. This can also be seen in the Native American cultures of North America. Each tribe has a shaman, that is to say a spiritual medium, who is capable of calling down spirits.

This person also often holds the post of chief and he or she listens to people's worries and cures their illnesses. Shinto priests and priestesses are also thought to have had a similar role in the past. So the role of spiritual medium has existed since ancient times.

Everybody probably knows or has heard about this sort of spiritual possession. In general, people understand possession as a spiritual phenomenon wherein a good number of people can see a spirit entering a medium and expressing itself.

Contrary to this, I use the word *possession* in a wider sense, not referring simply to the kind of possession that everybody can see and understand. Possession is a state wherein a being from the Spirit World inhabits a person constantly [or for a limited period], and influences his or her thoughts and actions. Generally the word *possession* is thought to refer to the taking over of a body by a malicious or evil spirit, but gods can also enter people's bodies. So it actually refers to the state of being possessed by a spirit, be it good or bad.

The phenomenon of possession is not limited to the state of trance as experienced by a shaman calling down a spirit upon him, but also occurs in people who live their ordinary daily life while being constantly affected by a particular spirit. The spirits in the other world can be roughly divided into those who live in Hell and those who live in Heaven, so the affecting spirit can be good or bad. Although the word *possession* is not generally used in this context, it can also refer to the state in which a person is receiving continuous advice from his or her guardian spirit. This is not exactly possession, but it is closely related.

The spirits in Hell cannot spend all their time possessing people on Earth. They will come to Earth when somebody is in a condition suitable for possession, but when this is no longer the case, spirits cannot stay. After they leave a person on Earth, these evil spirits return to their "domicile" in Hell, the place where they ought to be.

Hell is divided into numerous realms such as the Hell of Hungry Spirits, the Hell of Beasts, the Hell of Lust, the Hell of Strife [Asura Realm], and so on, and most of the spirits return to the particular area where they belong. When a person on Earth is emitting negative thoughts, however, the spirits return to possess and whisper in his or her ear.

On the other hand, spirits in the heavenly realm have their own jobs in the other world. For instance, guardian spirits look after their soul siblings living on

Earth, but they too have their own work and their own lives in the other world, so generally they only come to Earth when they feel that their advice is necessary. Therefore, although spirits may be here on Earth for a certain time, they will most likely be gone after a while. There are times when spirits are possessing and when they are not.

Overshadowing—
Two or three spirits can exist simultaneously

Possession is when a spirit comes to someone's body and influences the soul dwelling within it. When the two spirits overlap one another and influence the person, it is called "overshadowing." Possession works like a shadow, with the spirit covering the soul from above. That is why it is called "overshadowing."

If the tendencies of the soul of the possessed person and the possessing spirit are very similar, they can remain overlapping one another. Sometimes three spirits can coexist within a single body.

Members of Happy Science often watch videos of my lectures at a local branch and they sometimes notice that light suddenly appears in a flash around my head. An aura of golden light, four to eight inches wide, glows around me. It does not shine continuously, rather it flashes occasionally while I am speaking. Sometimes a disk of golden light, like a golden tray, appears out of my side, or a column of light descends and sits on my head.

I am sure that many people will experience this while watching my lectures. If you look closely, you will see the golden light flashing off and on. This is what is called a halo and this golden light appears when a supporting spirit comes down to overlap my own spirit body. When the golden column appears over my head, it means that a ray of light has descended from the heavenly realm. This is how people can see the light coming down onto me.

Thus, two or three spirit bodies can coexist in the same space, influencing one another.

3

Possession Occurs
When There is a Connection

The Law of Same Wavelengths' Attraction

I am now going to explain further why possession occurs. One of the laws that I must definitely mention is the "The Law of Same Wavelengths' Attraction." We often use this term at Happy Science and I would like you all to understand it clearly.

While you are living on Earth, you are a three-dimensional being whose mind is confined in a physical body that belongs to this world. Your mind is the core of your soul, however, and is always connected with the world that exists beyond this one.

The mind can be described as being like an electromagnet, and the frequencies transmitted by the mind, or the tone of the mind, are in a state of constant exchange with the Spirit World, the two affecting and being affected by each other. The mind is connected to the Spirit World in this way.

The key to understanding possession lies with the mind: what is your mind attracting as an electromagnet? For instance, if you wish to know what kind of spirit is possessing you at the moment or what kind of spirit is likely to come to you, all you have to do is examine your mind. In most cases, you will be in contact with spirits that share the same type of thoughts that fill your mind.

This Law of Same Wavelengths' Attraction is quite difficult to comprehend, but once you gain actual experience, it is very easy to tell what spirits possess you. I often explain this law as being similar to changing the channels on a television.

The broadcasting companies send out various programs, but if the television is not tuned to them, the image cannot be seen; however, when it has been properly tuned to a channel, the image becomes quite clear. The same is true of the radio. If it is properly tuned in, if it is on the correct wavelength, then the FM programs can be heard, but if the frequencies do not match, you will hear nothing.

This is also how your mind works. Various kinds of "broadcast wavelengths" are emitted from the realms of Heaven and Hell, but if people on Earth are not tuned in, they will not be able to receive such signals.

In the United States there is an institute called SETI [Search for Extraterrestrial Intelligence], which searches all the electromagnetic signals that come in through radio telescopes, in an effort to find those that have been produced artificially. They have been investigating these signals for several decades now. There are a vast number of signals that come in all the time from space, however, and it is very difficult for them to pinpoint those that might have been produced by intelligent life, although in recent years there was a small news article saying that they had succeeded in detecting some.

Similarly, there is a vast diversity of signals and messages emanating from all kinds of beings throughout the Spirit World. When the wavelength exactly matches that of somebody on Earth, spirit and human become attuned to one another. When spirits are in contact in this way or when a spirit is needed on Earth, it is possible for the spirit to visit Earth.

If you know the name of a spirit, You can contact it

The Spirit World is so vast that, even after you return there, it can be very difficult to meet people. It is so big that it is difficult to know where someone is. You have no way of knowing if the one you wish to meet is above you, below you, distant, or close by.

So how do you get into contact with someone you wish to meet in the Spirit World? Of course, you will gradually be drawn toward the spirits and places that emit similar frequencies, or retain a similar state of mind to yours. The attraction of the same wavelength will pull you toward a certain world or village, and you will enter a place to which you are most suited, a place that suits the frequency and state of your mind.

Moreover, if you are acquainted with someone and know his or her name, all you have to do is to call out that name and your mind will connect to him or her right away. If you know a person's face, it is even easier to make a connection and you can get in contact immediately.

The same is true when people in this world try to get in touch with an inhabitant of the Spirit World. If you do not know the names of spirits, then it is very difficult to reach them. Conversely, if the spirits reveal their names to people on Earth, then they will receive many thoughts from various people. Therefore spirits are very reluctant to reveal their true names.

The deities or gods that appear in the various religions here on Earth generally keep their true identity secret and use different names, but this is not necessarily because they wish to deceive people. In the same way that anybody can contact you if they know your telephone number, in the other world, all it takes is a name and an idea of who someone is to start making contact. This can be very hard on the spirits.

Therefore spirits try to avoid people who do not have a proper introduction. They do not want just anybody to be able to contact them, so most gods, whether they are Shinto or of other religions, prefer to keep their names hidden. Sometimes they may agree to guide somebody using their true name, but in many cases they use a different name to hide their true form. If the spirits allow their form or name to be known, it becomes possible for people on Earth to contact them, but if they keep their name secret, then people will be unable to communicate with them. This is the way it is.

If you have some kind of affinity or connection with certain spirits, for example, your mind is emitting the same frequency as they are, or you are acquainted with them or you know their names, then you will be able to attune yourself to them. This is the Law of Spiritual Connection. You need some connection to attune to a spirit.

Places where you can be connected To the Spirit World

Of course, you can also create a spiritual connection through a place. For instance, people may go to pray at a shrine or visit a grave and create a spiritual connection with a certain spirit. If you create a connection through a certain place in this way, you can be connected to that spirit.

The Spirit World is a vast place and, as I mentioned, if you wish to contact a certain spirit, you need either to attune yourself to the same frequency or know that spirit. It is the same as on Earth where you can easily contact someone if you know their telephone number. If you are able to identify the spirit, you will be able to reach it.

There are also places that are connected to a particular spirit, places where you can reach a spirit if you go there. For example, the island of Shikoku in Japan has numerous temples on it, and many of them are famous as part of the eighty-eight temple pilgrimage. The temples have large grounds with a building in the center where the statue of Buddha is placed, and people go there and pray to the statue. These temples act like a telephone operator, linking this world with the Spirit World.

People with psychic ability are able to communicate with spiritual beings in the other world without visiting such places, but temples and religious sites usually work as instruments receiving the will of spirits to communicate with the people in this world.

For example, Shinto shrines are often used for weddings. During weddings, when the Shinto priests intone prayers, the gods of matchmaking really come down to celebrate the couple and psychics are able to feel their presence most strongly. This is the true form of religious work. The same can also be said of Christian weddings. I believe Christian angels also come down to bless a couple. When this kind of service is held, these spirits usually come.

Spiritual beings will come down to designated places or religious magnetic fields that are connected to them. For this reason, the phenomenon of possession frequently occurs during religious ceremonies. When large numbers of people gather at such ceremonies, which include dancing and festivities, the participants have high expectations of a visit from the spirits. Also, because it is a festival, many "invitations" are sent out to the Spirit World and large numbers of the spirits of ancestors and deities find it very easy to visit Earth.

Generally, the spirits are busy with their jobs in the Real World and do not have the time to come down to Earth, but when there is a festival where large numbers of people gather, expectations run high and they come. On these occasions, divine possession is quite common.

Many spiritual phenomena Are caused by bad spirits

So far I have explained that possession occurs easily when the person is on the same wavelength as a spirit, when the person knows the spirit's name or appearance, or when a person visits a place designated for the spirit. Related to the latter situation, it is generally also easy for possessions to occur within a religious organization.

There are all kinds of religions in this world. As some religious sects are connected to Heaven and others are connected to Hell, it is a bit of a gamble as to which a person should believe in. If they select the wrong one, there is a good chance that they will be possessed by a bad spirit.

Among religious sects where many spiritual phenomena occur, there are those that are connected to evil. If somebody joins and trains in such a group, even people who are not prone to being possessed by evil spirits will become possessed. These religious groups are home to large numbers of bad spirits, and by visiting and deepening their relationship with such spirits, people become possessed.

Religious groups that focus on spiritual phenomena attract a plethora of spirits including human spirits, animal spirits, and others. It can be quite dangerous sometimes, so to keep yourself out of trouble, it is best not to get involved with such groups.

In Japan there is a religious group that is notorious for being a misguided religion. Despite this, it retains some followers. There are between several hundred and a thousand followers and the reason for this is clear. The members have experienced some kind of spiritual phenomenon and they take this to be proof of the validity of their group.

Spiritual phenomena sometimes occur when people train in groups in a religion. When large numbers of people join together to recite mantras, pray, or meditate, their bodies will sometimes move of their own volition as a result of spiritual phenomena. Their hands may move, their bodies may hop around, go limp, move back and forth sideways or vertically; they may not be able to leap, but they may begin to bounce up and down.

When they undergo this kind of experience, they will feel grateful and believe that it proves their religion is a true one. People who have experienced such phenomena will be reluctant to leave their faith.

On Earth, people are so ill informed about spiritual matters that once they have experienced a spiritual phenomenon, many will quickly believe that it is the power of God or Buddha. However, the most common forms of spiritual phenomena experienced on Earth are caused by stray spirits. Vast numbers of spirits that could not return to Heaven remain lurking on Earth and these are always the ones that approach a person first.

If a spirit enters somebody with little training and whose mind is not in a good state, then it is most likely to be a spirit that has failed to return to Heaven. If a large number of these phenomena occur within a group, then it is safe to say that bad spirits are involved. If a person has trained properly for a long time, then they may encounter good spirits, but the spiritual phenomena that happen easily in a group of people are generally brought about by bad spirits.

These spirits are lost and seeking salvation. They visit such religions wanting to be saved. In the same way that people come to a religion in search of salvation, so do spirits. When stray spirits come across a group of people praying, the spirits quickly possess the people. Possessed by a spirit, the believer thinks that God has come down to him or her and feel grateful. The spirit enjoys being revered in this way and feels that it has been saved.

Thus the possessor feels good, as if it is doing a good deed, while the possessed feels that he or she is no longer an ordinary person but in some way superhuman. Both become rapturous with joy, mistakenly believing themselves to be saved.

Moreover, after joining this sort of religious group, sometimes the spirit that originally possessed a person is driven out by a new spirit. When this happens, that person may suddenly be cured of an illness. The first spirit to possess the person may have caused them to become sick, but when a bigger spirit forces the first spirit out, the person may be cured. When this happens, the person concerned becomes even more convinced of their faith. In this way, even evil religions are sometimes capable of curing disease.

4

Attachments Attract Spirits from Hell

Animal spirits possess
At the acupuncture points of the body

In times of sickness, the part of the physical body that is damaged is often damaged in the spirit body as well. According to Eastern medicine, there are various acupuncture points in the body, located in areas such as the head, neck, shoulders, back, lower back, legs, and so on, which are used in massage, acupuncture, and moxa. These acupuncture points coincide with the parts of the body that animal spirits tend to possess.

A spirit can possess a body when there is something to attach itself to. When somebody's blood flow is disrupted and congested in a certain area, spirits are able to latch onto it. The places where this congestion occurs become prone to fatigue or pain and, looked at spiritually, they take on a dark shadow. This is where a spirit can attach itself.

For instance, people suffering from rheumatism or who say that their feet always feel cold often have a snake spirit wrapped tightly around their legs. Those who suffer from chronic headaches, who are always complaining that their head hurts, often have an animal spirit possessing their head. Spiritually, at a glance, you might think that they have a scarf tied around their head, but on closer inspection, you will see it is a long snake. It could also be the spirit of a fox or something similar that is holding the person's head with its front paws. People who are always complaining of headaches may have an animal spirit riding on them and pressing down on their head.

People who continually suffer from abnormally sore shoulders or pains in the neck may also have the spirit of an animal riding on them. The same is true for pain in the small of the back. Spirits can possess different parts of the body.

What kind of mind is prone to possession?

Then, why do spirits possess your body at the acupuncture points? When you are possessed, a part of your spirit body is also in pain, but the reason for the pain is actually to be found in your mind.

I spoke earlier of the Law of Same Wavelengths' Attraction, and there is always a reason why a spirit possesses a body. The spirit cannot possess the person without any reason. For a spirit to possess somebody, both the possessor and the possessed must share the same mind; their minds must be of the same quality. So what kind of mind does a spirit tend to possess?

As you can imagine, Hell is a damp, dark place where the light of Heaven does not reach, where the Spiritual Sun does not shine. On the other hand, it is always daytime in Heaven because the Spiritual Sun is always shining down upon it. The spirits living in Heaven live by absorbing its light as their energy.

The skies of Hell are always covered with heavy rain clouds. These clouds are made of evil thoughts created by the inhabitants of Earth and Hell. No matter how bright the light may be, if the clouds are thick enough, the light will not be able to penetrate them. In this way, the clouds of evil thoughts spread out and cut off the light, leaving it dark below. Symbolically, Hell is like a cave in a mountain or an underground world. The realm of Hell is a place where the sun does not shine.

What kind of mind does not receive light? It is a mind that stands in opposition to the light. When your mind opposes the light, it reacts by creating clouds. Then, what kind of mind stands in opposition to the light? For living people, it is a mind that is consumed with worries and troubles. Worries and troubles cause the mind to be in a dark, negative state.

As long as you are living on Earth as a human, it is impossible to avoid worries altogether. Everybody has worries, but as long as you have the ability to resolve your worries and problems, you will be all right. If you are unable to solve your problems, however, your mind will become shackled. Your mind becomes bound to one spot and you cannot stop thinking about the problem.

If this state continues for a long time, that is to say, your thoughts remain fixed on a single issue, then it will appear to spirits in Hell as if a rope has been lowered down to them from above. They will look at this single, long rope and say to themselves, "What is this rope in front of me? I suppose someone wants me to come up." They will then grasp hold of it and begin to climb. They will approach the person with the worries as if to offer help. So if you constantly worry about one issue for a long period of time, spirits from Hell will start to visit you.

People who want to commit suicide Attract the spirits of people who killed themselves

Recently, we have seen an upsurge in the number of suicides. In particular, we have seen an increase in the number of company presidents whose businesses have floundered, who are unable to recover no matter how hard they try, who fail to run a new venture, or who cannot get backing from the banks and end up taking their own lives. There was even a man in Japan who left a major bank to become the CEO of another bank that had caused various social problems and, unable to overcome the difficulties faced by the bank, he hung himself.

I am sure that they were not bad people, but their worries remained focused on one problem that they were unable to solve. When this happens, the worry creates vibrations of pain that attract spirits who are on the same wavelength. Spirits that resonate with these vibrations are able to connect with the person.

When a company president is considering taking his own life, the spirits of other presidents who have already committed suicide will come to him. There are company presidents who died one, two, ten, even twenty years earlier and have been languishing in Hell or who never made it to Hell but still haunt their old company or home. Such spirits latch onto the feelings of people who are struggling in a similar situation and come to them.

The spirits may believe they are consoling and supporting somebody who is suffering with the same problems they did, but in actual fact, they are not helping them, but are trying to drag them down into the other world. Looked at objectively, the spirits are dragging the living down into the same morass in which they are trapped, to increase the number of fellow sufferers.

These spirits do not necessarily act out of malice when dragging their victims into the other world; they are just completely lost. Their mere presence amplifies the emotion of sadness and worry in the living, however, causing them further anguish and confusion. Their presence will cause people to lose all hope for the future and choose to die.

Religion teaches the way
To overcome worries and pain

Worries and pain are something that everybody experiences in life and, since ancient times, religion has taught ways to overcome them. If worries and pain are held for an extended period, they develop into attachments that are impossible to escape. If such worries remain for a long time, they can become dangerous. Therefore you must abandon attachments and release your mind from such worries.

The ways to overcome them are, for example, praying to Buddha or God, and practicing self-reflection. You can also learn the Buddhist teaching of impermanence, that everything belonging to this world, everything with a physical form, perishes eventually. This means that your house will eventually crumble and you will be parted from your loved ones. Your thoughts may now be consumed by your company or work, but even this company cannot last forever. You must realize that all things in this world are transient and impermanent.

While the previous may appear to be a rather pessimistic outlook, the principle of impermanence allows you to get rid of the greed for fame, the self-serving greed to expand your business, and all other earthly attachments. As a result, you will feel somewhat relieved and the possessing spirits will move away. You must stop thinking in ways that amplify your worries.

Another method is to think positively, to make your heart brighter, and to cut your connections with evil spirits. Different religions use different approaches to help people.

To sum up, if you hold on to worries for a long time, you will eventually attune yourself to evil spirits and attract them to you. Evil spirits who have a similar mind state as you will come and possess you. For example, if you are suffering with a business matter, you may find the spirit of a dead company president possessing you and sharing your worries and suffering, believing it is his own company.

5

The Increase of Unhappiness Caused By Spirits Unable to Return to Heaven

There are spirits who do not realize they are dead

Large numbers of people die in the cancer wards of hospitals. I wonder whether such facilities are good or bad because the people who have died in these wards and are unable to return to Heaven most likely remain in these buildings. I am sure there are large numbers of these sorts of stray spirits.

When a new patient is brought in, these stray spirits think, "Ah, a new guest has arrived," and then, possessing the patient, they go through the experience of death again with the patient. In this way, spirits repeat the cycle of possession and death endlessly.

I presume there are hospital wards that have become a form of Hell. These spirits have no idea how to break away from this cycle of pain on their own. They do not know that the other world exists and that it is based on logical rules, so they remain attached to this world, to physical bodies, determined not to "die."

These people have already died of cancer and no longer have physical bodies, but they do not understand this. They do not understand because they did not learn anything about life after death in school and, unless they have studied religion, they have no idea about it. As a result, they believe they are still alive because they have consciousness. To them, as long as they retain consciousness, it must mean that they are alive.

Moreover, because they can see the hospital ward, they think that they are still under the care of the hospital. They do not think that they are dead. Assuming that they are still patients, they get angry that the nurses and doctors are ignoring them and that a new patient has taken over their bed. The spirits of the dead find themselves in a miserable situation in which they live together with the living.

It is important to believe in a righteous religion

By changing one's state of mind, it is possible to get rid of possessing spirits. However, possession continues to occur in this world because there are currently countless spirits who are unable to return to Heaven after they die. This is a major problem. So if religions are lacking power, it is quite problematic. If religions are powerless, the world will be filled with people who do not have a basic understanding of the truth.

Different types of people die in hospitals. For example, there are people with a good educational background or high social status and others who do not have these things. There are also people who are rich and people who are not. But in death they are all equal and, at the time of death, everybody is dealt with in the same way. After death, no one is treated in a special manner and salvation will not come immediately to those who have not attained a certain level of enlightenment.

The first level of enlightenment is to grasp the truth that human beings are not physical bodies but are essentially spiritual beings. I presume that about 70 percent of people have not attained this first level of enlightenment. There may be some who have a vague understanding or some slight belief in it, but there are very few who are deeply convinced of it and believe that it actually applies to themselves. This really is a problem.

Therefore it is extremely important that you believe in and are devoted to a righteous religion while you are still alive. If you do, you will be able to find salvation quite quickly after death. You will, of course, find the spirits who work to assist the dead coming to help you in the other world. Then, all you need to do after returning to the next world is to change the habits you had when living in a physical body to those fitting for a spiritual being, although this change of mind-set is a little difficult.

Spirits who cause trouble for their families
After an unexpected death

It is not easy for people who die unexpectedly, without any spiritual knowledge or a certain level of spiritual awareness, to depart this world for the next. People who die of illness may be more or less aware of their death, but those who die suddenly, for example, in a traffic accident, will find it very difficult to accept their death.

They have been eager to live for ten or twenty more years, and if they still have their career and family, it is understandable that they cannot easily abandon their attachment to life in this world. They will naturally worry about their young children, their spouse, or their business, so even if they are told to abandon their worries, they cannot help but worry.

Their minds are focused on such problems, so they end up back at their home. In most cases, the spirits of the dead live inside the house with their spouse and children. They only want to fix the situation and often do not realize that their presence is actually exerting a negative influence on their family. Although they may be worrying about their spouse, children, or grandchildren, the fact is that they remain attached to this world, possessing family members. They have nowhere else to go, as they do not know where to return to in the other world or they cannot stay forever in their grave.

When people are possessed by spirits who cannot return to Heaven, their bodies feel heavy and they do not feel well. Their worries are amplified, they are always concerned about the same problem, and they cannot feel positive. Spirits that cannot return to Heaven may mean no harm, but they unintentionally cause trouble by remaining on Earth.

Moreover, some spirits are even unaware of the fact that they are already dead. They are upset by the fact that, despite having returned home, none of their family members seems to notice their presence. Their children do not answer when they speak to them and their spouse also ignores them. So the spirits try hard to do something to be noticed, resulting in spiritual disturbance. The spirit thus creates misfortune and "bad news."

For instance, family members or descendants of the deceased may be injured, have an accident, or suddenly become ill. The spirit of the deceased often causes misfortune in this way so that the family will realize something is wrong and start to suspect that the deceased is lost and has returned to this world. Some people find it strange that they are suddenly confronted with a rash of unfortunate incidents and visit the local branch of Happy Science to consult.

The spirit of the deceased cannot do anything good so it does something bad because it is easy to do. So there are times when a spirit sends various signals. They do such things simply because they have not attained a certain level of enlightenment nor been aware of the spiritual truth. As a result, while the spirit concerned has no intention of causing problems, they create further misfortune and increase unhappiness.

Malicious spirits
Who intentionally make people unhappy

It is too much to call these poor spirits "malicious spirits," so I usually call them "bad spirits" or "evil spirits." In this way, there are bad spirits and good spirits. "Bad spirits" sound less threatening, while "malicious spirits" suggest a sense of being consciously bad and vengeful. Just as the term suggests, the latter actively curse people. These spirits are more persistent than bad spirits. They are aware that they are lost spirits and they intentionally curse and haunt people.

They actively create misfortune in this world and destroy happiness. They try to bring suffering to people on Earth because they cannot find happiness of their own. They know only how to hold grudges and strive to make people unhappy. For instance, there are the spirits of people who did not do well in business, whose companies went bankrupt and who committed suicide. They know that their company is done for, but if nothing else, they at least want to destroy companies belonging to their friends in the same way. They also wish to bring misery to relatives who laughed at their failure.

In this way, if spirits start seriously and purposely to try and make others suffer, they will be classified as "malicious spirits." If they are left to their own devices, they will carry out evil deeds endlessly, one after another.

To a greater or lesser extent, everybody has the feeling, "If I cannot be happy, then I want other people to be unhappy too." No one can deny this. If you cannot be successful and find happiness yourself, then you will want to make others unhappy as well, to feel better. This feeling can build up and, eventually, it becomes a powerful force.

However, it is pitiful to see people living ordinary lives here on Earth who, upon leaving this world in a few years or decades, will turn into such miserable beings in the next life.

Materialistic people cannot save themselves After death

Several years ago, there was a movie called *The Sixth Sense*. A psychiatrist is killed, but he continues to analyze a small child, believing he is still alive. One day, however, he finally realizes that he is dead and is, in fact, a ghost.

Just as this movie portrays, even psychiatrists are unable to recognize their own death. They only have materialistic knowledge, so they believe that any negative symptom can be explained as a fault in the brain or the effect of drugs. So, even if they were to die, they would not be able to save themselves. This is not a joke, as it actually happens sometimes.

In addition to psychiatrists, there are probably many philosophers who will be unable to help themselves when they die. People who believe that they are intelligent and know all the truths of the universe do not usually listen to anybody else, so even if somebody comes to help them, they cannot be saved.

Not only are there medical professors and philosophers who believe in materialism, there are even Buddhist scholars who do not believe in the next world or the existence of the soul. It is very difficult to help these people return to Heaven. Unfortunately, nothing much can be done about these kinds of people until they have undergone a full course in Hell.

In short, the beliefs they held while living on Earth were very far from the Truth. So they need to undergo numerous experiences until they thoroughly understand where they have been mistaken. Otherwise, they cannot be saved.

6
To Avoid Possession by Spirits from Hell

Abandon envy and complaint,
Live with a righteous mind

I have spoken about various issues in relation to spiritual possession. It is, of course, a good thing to be in touch with your guardian spirit or with angels. There are not so many people who are able to connect with higher beings like angels, but I think many people are able to communicate with at least their guardian spirit.

If you are connecting with spirits from Hell, however, it is a problem. Spirits from Hell drive people's lives to misfortune and increase the number of unhappy people, so we must put a stop to this type of possession phenomenon, at all costs.

As I explained earlier, possession takes place when the wavelengths of your mind are attuned to those of a spirit. So then, what kind of mind will attract evil spirits? What kind of mind can be described as a negative one?

There are numerous examples of a negative mind. There is, for example, an envious mind, a mind that is full of jealousy. There is a mind that is always filled with dissatisfaction and complaint. Then there is the kind of mind that is always slandering or abusing others, hurting people with negative words. There is also a cynical mind.

Also, there is a mind that suffers from a persecution complex. Those who are susceptible to spiritual possession generally suffer from a persecution complex. They believe that people are always bullying them, that they are being hurt or injured, and that they always lose out.

This type of thinking is usually accompanied by a mind that blames others. It is a mind that always believes that somebody else is at fault, always trying to put the blame on parents, friends, teachers, superiors at work, colleagues, lovers, the environment, their job, the economy, anything but themselves. They do not assume responsibility for the awful situation that they are in and continue blaming others. Spirits in Hell find it very easy to approach people like this who tend not to take responsibility for their own life.

Another kind of negative mind is an angry one. Everybody gets angry at times, but people who become angry on a regular basis, who are always in a rage, are generally in tune with Hell. People who are always angry, who are filled with unreasonable rage, will attract spirits from Hell.

People who easily lose their temper, who say and do terrible things, who complain, or who have a persecution complex, always blaming others for their misfortune, will be approached by spirits from Hell.

There is also the opposite type of mind. People with low self-image, low self-acknowledgment, low self-esteem, people who think that they are no good, a complete failure, that they are beyond help, and that they should have never been born, will also attract Hell spirits. Their minds are also covered with dark clouds.

The six worldly delusions: greed, anger, ignorance, Pride, doubt, and false views

According to the Buddhist doctrine, the main factors that create a negative mind can be summed up as the six worldly delusions, which are greed, anger, ignorance, pride, doubt, and false views.

Greed is excessive desire. Everybody has desires, but if they are taken too far, it appears very ugly to others. When others see greedy people, they think, "He is too greedy. He is expecting big returns for the little work he does" or "She is trying to make money without doing anything."

In *samurai* movies, for example, we often see a corrupt local administrator defeated by a virtuous hero. In these stories, the evil administrator is generally greedy and willing to break the law to make unfair profits. These kinds of people have excessive greed.

The next delusion is anger. It is the kind of mind that suddenly flies into a rage, and people with this kind of mind are prone to possession by animal spirits, particularly snakes.

Next, we have ignorance, or foolishness. This refers

to the kind of people who make many mistakes and create their own suffering. In particular, there is ignorance with regard to religious truth. There are many people who claim the opposite of religious truth, who believe the opposite of what I teach. They think that worldly pleasure is everything and immerse themselves in it.

Fools are people who do not seek any spiritual values but seek happiness only through material objects or physical pleasure. This is what is meant by ignorance. There are plenty of foolish people even among those who have a high IQ and are able to excel in their studies at school. The pain created by this ignorance attracts the spirits of Hell.

Pride is the conceited heart, or the arrogant mind. This is similar to the mind of *tengu** [long-nosed goblins] who are forever boasting of their power. Tengu do not necessarily belong in Hell, but in many cases their conceit brings them down and makes them suffer. This suffering, in turn, creates a road to Hell. Conceit is a shortcut to failure and there are many people who fail as a result of conceit.

The next delusion is doubt. In this context, I am generally referring to a mind that doubts Buddha's

---

* *Tengu* are beings who live in the mountains of the Tengu Realm in Minor Heaven, or the back side of Heaven. They like to boast about their strength and focus solely on strengthening their physical and psychic powers for their own interest. For more information, please refer to Ryuho Okawa, Chapter 3, Section 4 of *The Nine Dimensions* (IRH Press, 2012).

Truth, but it also includes suspicion, a tendency to doubt others, and a defiant heart.

The last delusion, false views, refers to mistaken ideologies and outlooks. There are numerous mistaken outlooks, and some of them are taught in schools. There are mistaken political and economic ideologies and also mistaken ideas taught in various organizations or religious groups.

Once you become obsessed with a mistaken idea, once it has entered your head, you will see everything from the opposite perspective. For this reason, it will be extremely difficult for somebody who is a member of a misguided religion, who believes in wrong ideologies, to attain enlightenment. They must at least leave the organization to achieve that. In the same way that it is hard to achieve enlightenment while in a gang of robbers, it is difficult to find the Truth while amongst people who believe in a false ideology.

There are many false views in the world today; even among intellectuals, false views are extremely common. The worst disseminator of false views is journalism. The world is being flooded with mistaken ideas through the reports that appear in the newspapers, on television, in weekly magazines and the like. As a result, confusion is created on Earth and Hell expands itself, creating a large number of inhabitants. This kind of occurrence is common.

You should think of greed, anger, ignorance, pride, doubt, and false views as basic examples of a negative mind. In addition, on an emotional level, sudden rage, complaining, and putting the blame on others denote a negative mind. Somebody whose words and actions are bad and whose lifestyle is disorderly can also be said to have a negative mind.

Commit yourself to a healthy lifestyle

To approach the problem from a different angle, an unhealthy lifestyle is another major factor in attracting evil spirits. Therefore it is also important that you lead a regular and orderly life, and allow your body to rest. Even if you are living with a right mind, if you become exhausted, it will be difficult for heavenly spirits to approach you. In fact, if you are too tired, evil spirits will be attracted and find it easier to possess you. So living a healthy lifestyle can protect you from evil spirits.

In order to keep away evil spirits, willpower is necessary. You cannot fight off evil spirits without having a certain level of willpower. Moreover, it is beneficial for increasing your spiritual power.

In Eastern medicine, there are various plants that are said to have the power to increase vitality and spiritual power, such as garlic, ginseng, and so on. These have a certain efficacy because they themselves contain spiritual energy. If you take these, you will quickly gain energy. It is not good to rely on these aids for too long, however.

When you are physically exhausted, you will find that light does not enter your body, but evil is easily attracted instead, and you will be unable to correct your mind, no matter how hard you try. Therefore, when you are feeling exhausted, it is important that you first return to a healthy lifestyle. Take a rest, eat nutritiously, and rebuild your body. Unless you regain your health, it may be impossible to get rid of evil influences.

In this way, to avoid possession by evil spirits, it is important to live with the righteous mind and follow a healthy lifestyle.

Create a spiritual screen
To prevent the entry of evil spirits

Religions often talk of creating a spiritual screen or barrier. If you are fighting with evil spirits on your own, your mind can be connected to various realms in the Spirit World according to the laws of the mind. That is why it is important that you create a good spiritual field to prevent evil spirits from intruding.

For instance, the Shinto religion stretches a sacred straw rope across the entrance of the place where their gods are worshiped. By doing so, they create a sanctuary, protecting themselves with a barrier that the evil spirits are unable to cross.

Sumo wrestling is essentially an event dedicated to the gods and so a grand champion also wears one of these sacred ropes. The way in which the ring itself is circled by a thick straw rope indicates a kind of barrier as well.

The sumo wrestlers also sprinkle salt on the ring before each bout, an act that symbolizes purification. In the Shinto religion, salt is said to have the power to drive away evil spirits and, as sumo is part of divine service, the wrestlers sprinkle salt on the ring. When they sprinkle the salt, wrestlers sometimes lick it. Licking salt causes the body to heat up, acting as a defense against negative vibrations and evil spirits.

When the wrestlers go up into the ring, they go naked, symbolizing the fact that they are hiding nothing. Sumo that is staged at festivals is a religious ceremony where wrestlers show that they are disciplining themselves with a good mind that is praiseworthy from the perspective of the gods.

Sometimes various female counselors and ministers have wanted to enter the ring, but the Sumo Federation does not permit it, saying that sumo is a divine service and a religious ceremony. They say that if a woman were to enter the ring, it would bring earthly desires, causing wrestlers to think about women and preventing them from wrestling well. Such rules have a religious significance.

This, of course, has nothing to do with sexual prejudice. Priestesses working in the Shinto shrines, who play a supportive role in the religious ceremonies, are mostly unmarried women in their teens. A god could only come down to a passive subject. As the vibration of women is very gentle, they make ideal subjects. Untainted women have a very soft vibration, creating an atmosphere of great passivity and making it easier for the gods to come down.*

Men, on the other hand, tend to be more active and are good at employing willpower. For this reason, when conducting a prayer requiring strong willpower, such as prayers to drive away or exorcise evil spirits, it is usually better to gather men; in this way, the power can easily be focused.

When calling down a god from Heaven, however, it is better to do it through a woman. It is best to have one who is pure, so, since ancient times, it has been a custom at shrines to use unmarried women or women who have few worries.†

---

* Yanagita also speaks of "women's emotivity" on page 254 of *Imoto-no-Chikara* [The Power of Sisters], which is included in his *Yanagita Kunio Zenshu 11* [The Complete Works of Kunio Yanagita, Vol. 11] (Chikuma Shobo).

† On pages 168-169 of *Miko-ko-no 4* [Thoughts on Priestess 4], in *Yanagita Kunio Zenshu 24* (Chikuma Shobo), he writes: "The role of the priestesses is not necessarily confined to women....it is not unheard-of for men to play it," but this is an exception.

But even if a woman is a priestess, she is sometimes not allowed to go inside the barrier during her monthly period. At this time, she is losing a lot of blood and her body aches, so her spiritual power decreases, her aura fades, and her mind is prone to worries. At such times, she is unable to assist fully in calling down the gods and she may be asked to stay away. This is how religions have worked since ancient times.

I am often targeted by enemies who work actively to interfere with my mission, in other words, by devils and malicious spirits. That is why I have to create a systematic line of defense against them. In order to achieve this, I create a spiritual force field that is protected by a spiritual screen upheld by my disciples who train themselves. My family members are also creating a barrier, so I am guarded by two or three lines of defense.

There are many spirits who actively try to hinder me and, to prevent them from succeeding, I have to make a systematic defense. This can be achieved through personal spiritual discipline as I have stated, as well as by the use of a spiritual screen.

The local branches of Happy Science are also protected by a spiritual screen. Believers come to visit and take part in ceremonies in the prayer rooms. A kind of spiritual aura guards the local branches. Naturally, this is also true of our head temple, *Shoshinkan* in

Utsunomiya, and other main temples and *shojas*. They are surrounded by a kind of barrier.

In the home, if the whole family believes in Happy Science, if they recite our fundamental sutra, *Buddha's Teaching: The Dharma of the Right Mind*, watch my lecture videos, listen to my lecture CDs, read books of truth, and practice self-reflection, then a barrier will be created around the house, making it difficult for evil spirits to enter. The house will become a kind of fortress to protect your family from the outside world.

To sum up, in order to prevent possession by evil spirits, it is important that you first maintain harmony in your own mind and look after your physical health. Then, in order to maintain your defenses for a long time, you should work together with your Dharma friends and other believers to protect yourself. In particular, you should create a spiritual screen in your local branch, in your temple, and in your own home that will prevent evil spirits from entering. This is a very important thing to do and it is a good idea to protect yourself in a systematic way.

In this chapter, "The Principle of Spiritual Possession," I have explained the subject of possession from various perspectives. There is plenty more to be said on the subject, but I have tried to focus on a few important subjects. I hope that this chapter will help you advance on your path to enlightenment.

[Bibliography – Chapter Two]
- Mircea Eliade, *The Sacred and the Profane—The Nature of Religion*
- Mircea Eliade, *Shamanism: Archaic Methods of Ecstasy* (Bollingen Series)
- William James, *The Varieties of Religious Experience* (Routledge)
- Toji Kamata, *Shukyo-to-Reisei* [Religion and Spirituality] (Kadokawa Sensho)
- Kunimitsu Kawamura, *Hyoi-no-shiza, Miko-no-Minzoku-gaku II* [Aspects of Possession: Folklore Studies of the Shamaness II](Seikyu-sha)
- Rudolf Otto, *Das Heilige* [The Idea of the Holy](Oxford University Press)
- Kokan Sasaki, *Hyorei-to-Shaman* [Possession and Shaman] (University of Tokyo Press)
- Kokan Sasaki, Shamanism (Chuko Shinsho)
- Kokan Sasaki and Toji Kamata, *Hyorei-no-Ningengaku* [The Anthropology of Possession](Seikyusha)
- Noriyuki Ueda, *Sri Lanka-no-Akuma-barai* [Devil Exorcism in Sri Lanka](Tokuma Shoten)
- G. van der Leeuw, *Einfuhrung in die Phanomenologie der Religion* (Introduction to Religious Phenomena)
- Yasuo Yuasa, *Shukyo-keiken-to-Shintai* [Religious Experience and the Body](Iwanami Shoten)

Please note, however, that these works were not quoted or referred to directly in the writing of this book.

Chapter Three

The Principle of Channeling

~ For Receiving and Spreading Light ~

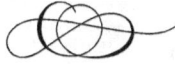

Lecture given on January 12, 2004

1

A Grand Plan Prepared 150 Years Ago

1848 — The beginning of spiritualism

In this chapter, I would like to talk about the principle of channeling. Happy Science began with automatic writing and spiritual phenomena, so I think that many of my readers are familiar with the word *channeling*.

The movement to spread the Truth by means of channeling the spirit world started long before the establishment of Happy Science. In fact, there has been a grand plan in place for over 150 years. To be more precise, I could say that the year 1848 was critical.

This was the year Karl Marx [1818-1883] and Friedrich Engels [1820-1895] published *Manifesto of the Communist Party* and it became clear that there would be a trend toward materialism throughout the world. It was predicted that the Soviet Union and China would rise to power, and materialism would spread and dominate about half the globe. Therefore, around the same time, a battle was being waged to counteract materialism. Many kinds of spiritual phenomena began to occur in the United States resulting in the foundation of modern spiritualism. The year this began was 1848.

At first, spiritual phenomena began to occur at the Fox home on the outskirts of New York, around the two daughters of the family. These physical phenomena began with rapping sounds that could be heard coming from different places, such as the ceiling. As the family looked more deeply into this strange phenomenon, the rapping changed to more active poltergeist incidents, which came to be known as the Hydesville Rappings. Various kinds of spiritual phenomena continued to occur to the Fox family, and these attracted the attention of people all over the country.

From these beginnings, spiritual phenomena began to occur throughout the world, with many also being witnessed in London. For instance, there was the "table turning" phenomenon, where a table moved automatically when you placed your hand on it.

At that time, the participants of the séance were even able to communicate with the spirits by setting certain rules. For example, they would point at twenty-six letters of the alphabet in order, one at a time, and the spirit would rap at a certain letter. By continuing in this way, the spirits could spell out words and transmit messages. This method is similar to the Ouija board.

Besides this, there were many other physical phenomena caused by spirits, such as objects floating in the air. All this was done to demonstrate the fallacy of materialism. Usually, however, high spirits are not too involved with the physical phenomena of this world and they are not very skilled at them. The higher dimensions are a world of thought where no physical objects exist, so high spirits do not take much interest in causing physical phenomena on Earth.

When it comes to causing physical phenomena, spirits who live closer to this world are more skilled. Therefore, high spirits worked with these spirits to make something visible happen. They thought that unless the presence of spirits was demonstrated physically, people on Earth would not be able to accept their existence.

Stage one — Proving the existence of the Spirit World Through physical phenomena

From the late nineteenth to the early twentieth century, more than one hundred famous psychics appeared on Earth. Many psychics were sent to every corner of the globe. When humans began to make great advances in science and to make the spiritual movement compatible with the development of science, many physical psychic phenomena were made to happen.

The plan for the first stage was to create physical phenomena that would prove and make people realize the existence of something beyond the understanding of humans, that some power from an unknown world was at work. To accomplish this, physical phenomena were produced continuously over several decades. Some famous examples are as follows.*

Scientists such as Sir William Crookes [1832–1919], who is famous for inventing the Crookes tube, a kind of vacuum tube, did scientific research into spiritual phenomena and they succeeded in extracting ectoplasm, a kind of spiritual energy, from the human body and materializing it. This is similar to what we call a ghost, but it is a physical materialization.

With the help of a medium named Florence Cook [1856–1904], William Crookes conducted various experiments. For example, Florence would fall into a trance, allowing a female ghost called Katie King to materialize in human form. She appeared with skin, veins, and hair, just like a real woman, allowing Crookes to take several dozen photographs and carry out other experiments.

This is one of the examples wherein a phenomenon was proved to be true. Florence, the spiritual medium, was placed on a pair of scales and it was discovered that while the ghost was present in physical form, Florence's weight dropped dramatically. It was recorded that

---

* For further information, refer to the following: Hiroshi Yamakawa, *Kyoi-no-Shinrei-Gensho-o-Mita* [I Witnessed Amazing Spiritual Phenomena](Gakken); *Bankoku-Shinrei-Ko-shashin-shu* [Old Spirit Photographs of the World] by the same author (Nanpodo); Janet Oppenheim, *The Other World: Spiritualism and Psychical Research in England*, (Cambridge University Press); J. H. Hyslop, *Opening the Door of the Spirit World*; Chiyomatsu Tanaka, *Shin-Reiko-Shiso-no-Kenkyu* [New Studies on Spiritualism](Kyoei Shobo Publishing), etc.

her body weight dropped in direct proportion to the amount of matter used by the ghost.

Although Katie was a ghost, when she took on material form, she became the same as a human being, with veins and a beating heart, and it was possible to touch her body. When Katie told people to cut her hair, they were able to do so. They could cut her hair, but once they did, it immediately grew back. No matter how much they cut, it would grow again. The hair was subjected to a variety of tests, including analysis under a microscope, and it was discovered to be ordinary human hair. Katie would also rip the skirt she was wearing, but when she did so, new material would quickly appear to repair the damage. They carried out various experiments of this kind.

It all seems very strange, but such phenomena occurred to awaken people to the spirit world. These experiments were carried out repeatedly between 1872 and 1874, but they were not the first instances of events of this kind.

In the story of Christ's resurrection, we find the following episode: One of Jesus' disciples, Thomas, doubted Jesus' resurrection, saying, "Unless I see the nail marks in his hands and put my finger where the nails were, and put my hand into his side, I will not believe it." Then Jesus appeared in physical form and said, "Put your finger here; see my hands. Reach out your hand

and put it into my side." Upon seeing this, Thomas doubted no more and believed [John 20]. This story appears in the Bible and is undoubtedly an example of materialization. Such occurrences have happened in the past.

Other examples of spiritual experiments, such as levitation, also exist. Psychics have conducted experiments in which they would float in the air. There was one experiment in which a person exited from a window about forty feet above ground level, circled the building in midair and reentered through another window.

Investigators also tried to transmit the voice of a spirit. So it could not be claimed that they were employing ventriloquism, they extracted a small amount of ectoplasm from a human body and placed it in a megaphone, creating an artificial voice box. This allowed the spirit to speak directly through the megaphone.

Another phenomenon was to produce jewels or other objects out of thin air. Such experiments to attract objects were done many times. There was also the phenomenon of glowing objects, where several glowing objects were produced and flew through the air.

Experiments in telepathy were also carried out. The investigators sought to discover whether this ability was due to some spiritual agency or actual telepathic powers.

If telepathy was not a spiritual phenomenon, they tried to see whether the subject was receiving messages from a living person or whether telepathy was just the result of split personality.

This all happened about one hundred years ago, so perhaps not many people know about it today. But at the time, various organizations such as the Society for Psychical Research sprang up and they were devoted to the scientific investigation of the spirit world, apart from the world of faith. They conducted numerous experiments in materialization. All kinds of methods were used to prove the existence of the spirit world and a vast amount of data on the subject exists in both the United States and the United Kingdom.

In the United Kingdom, the author of the Sherlock Holmes stories, Sir Arthur Conan Doyle [1859-1930], was a keen researcher of the spirit world. Many famous American writers also carried out studies on the subject and spiritualism became something of a boom.

In the United States, the man who is known as the father of psychology, William James [1842-1910], used his position as a respected scholar to undertake extensive research into spiritual matters, though he described it quite vaguely. His brother, Henry James [1843-1916], wrote a ghost story entitled *The Turn of the Screw* [Wildside Press]. The United States also saw the appearance of people like Leonora Piper [1859–1950], a powerful medium who had the powers of second sight, telepathy, clairvoyance, and so on, and was able to produce various spiritual phenomena including spiritual messages.

So research into spiritual matters was carried out extensively about one hundred years ago and this was widely spread. Various physical phenomena were used in this first stage to prepare the way for the second stage.

Stage two—Spreading the philosophy of The Spirit World through channeling

The beginning of the twentieth century saw the end of the first stage and the start of the second. The second stage was to spread the philosophy of the spirit world through automatic writing and spiritual messages.

High spirits began to send down messages from the heavenly realm, which were recorded by mediums through automatic writing or as voice messages and published as books. In the United Kingdom, the spirit of an American Indian named Silver Birch communicated with a medium and his words were published under the title *Guidance from Silver Birch*, while in France in the late nineteenth century, *The Spirits' Book* was published by Allan Kardec [1804-1869]. Both sets of messages were transmitted from the same source. Many other books of spiritual messages were published in both East and West.

So in the second stage, detailed descriptions of the spirit world and the thoughts of high spirits were widely transmitted throughout the world in the form of books. This second stage corresponded with World War I and II on Earth, so the high spirits were very passionate about their mission to spread the philosophy of the spirit world.

Stage three— ### Curing diseases through spiritual healing

After that, the dominance of science continued to increase throughout the twentieth century and there were great advances in medicine as well. This created a powerful stronghold for those who refused to believe in religion or the spirit world, so there arose a pressing need to solve this issue.

It is generally accepted that Charles Darwin [1809-1882] formulated the theory of evolution, but another scientist, Alfred Wallace [1823-1913], arrived at the idea of evolution at approximately the same time. Wallace was a spiritualist and his studies were devoted to spiritualism. If Wallace had been recognized as the father of the theory of evolution, history would have been very different because his theory of evolution was based on spiritual truth.

Darwin received the credit for the theory of evolution, however, and merged it completely with materialism. This was one of the first errors that changed the course of events. The combined work of Marx and Darwin strengthened materialism, as it became a major trend in the world. In the meantime, continuous advances have been made in science and medicine.

I have explained that the first step in the spread of spiritualism was to use mediums, and the second was to carry out channeling. Then, at around this time, we entered the third stage, when a lot of diseases were cured through the use of spiritual powers. During the third stage, many people with incurable diseases were healed by spiritual means. This happened around the world and, after World War II, it became particularly widespread.

People started to use spiritual healing to cure those on whom doctors had given up, those who were thought to be incurable. It was a battle against materialism in the field of medicine. This was very difficult to carry on, however. In the modern medical system in Japan, for example, only doctors are allowed to cure disease, so it is very hard for religions to heal people.

To sum up, a grand experiment in civilization took place in three stages. In this way, over a period of one hundred years, various preparations were made in order to create the necessary foundations for the Truth to be spread in the second half of the twentieth century. I, too, was involved in this project from the very beginning. When the plan was first proposed in the mid-nineteenth century, I was working on it in the Real World.

Materialism has entered
Both Christianity and Buddhism

In the heavenly realm, Jesus Christ assisted in the preparations in Christian countries. In addition to enemies such as materialism or the belief in the omnipotence of science, there was also a movement within the church itself, claiming that spiritual phenomena stopped in the time of Christ.

This trend came about because the church leaders did not possess any spiritual powers, so, in a way, it could not be helped. Now the church believes that spiritual phenomena stopped in the time of Christ, and their stance is to deny all spiritual phenomena that have happened since.

Within Christianity, there were sects that incorporated spiritual phenomena into their beliefs, but the adherents were treated as heretics and suppressed. When spiritualism emerged in the nineteenth century, Christianity stood in adamant opposition to that as well, and looked upon it as an enemy. It may be similar to the hatred often seen between close relatives, but the Church of England, which was a natural ally and should have offered its support, also turned upon spiritualism, saying it was the work of the devil, and tried to wipe it out.

Enemies can exist even within religion and this causes endless trouble. Today the church still refuses to accept spiritualism openly; they offer it lukewarm support, but the truth is that they do not want to believe its teachings.

One reason is a jealousy between rivals. Spiritualism is similar to a "new religion" and those who are conservative will always try to defend themselves against popular new trends. Another reason is the fact that spiritual phenomena have been largely cut out of the Bible. If the Bible contained all the spiritual phenomena that occurred in the period it covers, then I am sure that people would be more open to the idea of spiritualism, but these were removed in the editing process, making it difficult for people in later years to understand spiritual matters.

Materialism has also infiltrated Buddhism. This trend had already started in India a few hundred years after the death of Shakyamuni Buddha. India has always been a philosophical country and Buddhism was turned into a kind of philosophy. Being a religion, it was only natural for Buddhism to teach spiritual matters, but there came a period when people did not understand this fact and interpreted the teachings in a philosophical way. As a result, Buddhism became somewhat like a study of logic that taught people how to debate. A large amount of materialistic thinking has been incorporated into it.

In Buddhist universities in Japan today, there are many academics who claim that Buddhism does not recognize the existence of spirits or souls. This is a lamentable situation. If Buddhism did not recognize spirits or souls, then that would cause serious problems. Whether you call it a soul, a spirit, a mental function, an intention, an immortal intellect, *alaya-vijnana* [a storehouse of consciousness], or Buddha nature, if there is no spiritual entity that continues after leaving the physical body upon death, then Buddhism is empty belief.

If there is no soul, then the teaching that "all things are transient" will become a materialistic teaching. It will simply mean that when something breaks, that is the end, when a person dies, that is the end. Even if people are taught to abandon attachments, if life is limited only to this world, then people will choose to live a life of pleasure until the physical death of the body.

The teachings will then take on the opposite meaning; people who do not understand spiritual matters will interpret them in this way.

Materialism has quite clearly found its way into both Buddhism and Christianity. Christians believe that spiritual phenomena may have happened in ancient times but no longer happen today and they cannot think any further about this topic. Therefore various spiritual phenomena were created not only to fight science and materialism, but also to fight the stultification and fossilization of religion, where only the outer form, not the true belief, remained.

In an effort to prevent the fossilization of Buddhism, high spirits created esoteric sects that focus on the mystical and magical power of religion, and placed great importance on spiritual power or phenomena. Humankind has entered an era when, although the population has been increasing, more and more people have lost sight of the truth. That was the twentieth century.

2

The Mission of El Cantare

1956 — The beginning of a spiritual century

According to the Theravada Buddhism of Southeast Asia, 1956 marked the two thousand five hundredth anniversary of the death of Shakyamuni Buddha and this fact was celebrated with massive services. This period can be considered a turning point.

According to astrology, 1956 also marked the dawning of the Age of Aquarius. In other words, it was the beginning of a spiritual century. As the year 1956 was an important juncture in history, I decided to be born on Earth at this time.

Approximately one week after Shakyamuni Buddha was born in India, his mother, Mahamaya, died of puerperal fever. So this time, instead of Mahamaya, Hermes' mother, Maia, was chosen to bear me.

I was reborn in 1956 and the start of this movement to spread spiritual truth was destined for 1981. The reason this date was set was that it was considered adequate time for me to accomplish my work at a certain level before the twentieth century ended. Even in the late eighties, however, I did not have sufficient power so I felt impatient while undergoing many hardships. But before the turn of the millennium, I somehow managed to make Happy Science stand out in the world and spread new teachings to large numbers of people.

El Cantare—
The united consciousness of Buddha and Christ

If you look at my teachings, it is clear that I have several missions to accomplish during this lifetime, but, by and large, my mission includes that of Buddha and Christ [the Savior]. My teachings talk a lot about Buddhist enlightenment, and at the same time, they strongly emphasize love like Jesus did. This is the plan I had all along.

So if you were to describe this being called El Cantare, the easiest way would be to say that El Cantare is the united consciousness of Buddha and Christ. El Cantare is a being that clearly demonstrates the Laws, the Truth, and a being that expounds Jesus' teachings of love and salvation. Both of these sides have come out strongly in this lifetime.

I also preach Hermes' philosophy of progress and prosperity in a contemporary form. These teachings have provided Happy Science with its underlying strength. However, the aspects of enlightenment and love appear very strongly.

I have not yet taught Rient Arl Croud's "Laws of the Universe." If I have the time and the opportunity before I return to Heaven, I will try to preach the Laws of the Great Universe, but if I were to do so at too early a stage, I do not think that people would be able to understand them. That is the reason I have not taught them yet.

There are several other Laws that I have not yet taught, but as far as teachings go, I have emphasized the teachings as both Buddha and Christ, so what I am trying to accomplish should be clear.

Christians looked on the end of the twentieth century as a major turning point. The French prophet, Nostradamus [1503–1566], said that the end of the century would be a time of great danger and many Christians believed this. In this sense, there have been many religions that taught of the coming of a new Messiah, a large number of which were Christian. Some people may think that the "advent of the Savior" would be an extremely good thing, but for Christians it signifies the coming of an era of great suffering.

The truth is that Christians believe that the Savior will not come unless we face the end of an era, the end of humankind. For them, the coming of the Savior is something to be feared; the Second Coming means that humankind will encounter terrible disasters. In the Bible, "The Revelation of Saint John the Divine" contains numerous terrifying prophecies that have been believed for the last two thousand years. Many people think that the Last Judgment and the Second Coming of Christ will occur at the same time. The Last Judgment is actually a story that takes place in the spirit world, but many people believe that it is about Earth.

In order to overcome these beliefs, I created a plan to bridge the East and West, bringing salvation to all. This was a plan to save people in these times. In the East, people would not be able to understand our movement unless it was couched in Buddhist terms, while in the West the teachings have to be understandable to Christians. In the light of my teachings, there will be those who think I resemble Buddha, while others will think that I resemble Jesus Christ. I am capable of appearing like both.

In past lectures, the spirit of Christ has spoken directly through me, so to some people, I appear to be the resurrection of Christ. Naturally, this is part of the message I wish to transmit. This is a plan that has been in progress for 150 years before this present stage.

3

The Difficulties of Channeling

The reason high spirits
Send their spiritual messages anonymously

When I first began my religious movement, I chose to introduce the spiritual messages of high spirits as an example of spiritual phenomena*.

The reaction of the public was varied, and there were people who commented, "The contents are wonderful, but I think that too many famous people are giving messages. Usually, only one person of that stature would appear." You can also say, "If more than one god appears, it becomes confusing and the teachings lose their unity. To begin with, it is difficult to believe that so many spirits are descending to give messages."

In the past, people had the same sorts of opinions about spiritual messages, so many high spirits often chose to communicate anonymously with people on Earth. The recipient of these messages would say, "I do not know who sent it, but I have received a message from a high spirit," and then try to prove its veracity by the content [for example, *Guidance from Silver Birch*]. In this kind of atmosphere, it was a courageous and challenging

---

* As of 2015, many spiritual message books by the author are available in English. See *spiritualinterview.com*

act for me to publish spiritual messages revealing the spirits' real names.

Spirits chose to send anonymous messages because if they gave their real name, people on Earth would make unnecessary efforts to try and prove their validity. No matter how hard people tried, however, they would never succeed in finding convincing proof that a message was indeed sent by a certain spirit. Nothing exists today that would allow people to check on someone who lived hundreds or even thousands of years ago. If the recipient devotes all their attention to this, the message will go to waste, so many spirits decided to send their messages either anonymously or using a false name.

High spirits do not limit the use of false names to sending messages. False names were also used when religions were founded in the nineteenth century in Japan. If spirits were to use their real names, people on Earth might not understand, so they used the names of different gods or spoke anonymously. This is very common in Japanese religions [for instance in Konkokyo, Tenrikyo, or Oomoto].

After returning to the Spirit World, People start forgetting about this world

When souls return to the spirit world, they do not remember every detail of their life on Earth. In fact, their memories gradually fade. This is only natural, as I am sure most people do not remember everything from their childhood.

If you saw a record of all your memories of kindergarten, you would be surprised at what it contained. The same can probably be said of your primary school years. As the years pass, you forget the names and faces of the friends and teachers you had at that time. You may remember some of the things that your teacher told you, but there will be much more that you have forgotten. If you meet your friends from that time, you may be surprised to hear stories you have long ago forgotten. As you get older, you gradually forget your memories.

The process of moving on to the other world is also the process of forgetting this one. To move on to the next world is to be "reborn," whereas to be born into this world is the equivalent of dying in the other world and being born afresh here. This world and the next are completely opposite.

When individuals are due to be born in this world, their friends in the other world gather and longingly bid them farewell. When they are born into this world, however, they forget everything and, as they grow, they develop an awareness of themselves as inhabitants of this world, building up their knowledge and their stock of experiences and memories. Eventually, they grow old, their bodies weaken, their memories fade, and, ultimately, they return to the other world.

When they arrive back in the spirit world, they are beginners again, like newborn babies. They have to learn everything about the spirit world from scratch, just like small children starting school. When they return to the other world, they take with them the essence of the experiences they had on Earth, but trivial memories are all left behind. If they were to remember everything, it would hinder their soul training in the other world.

From the viewpoint of the heavenly realm,
The body is like iron armor

The details of our life in this world are recorded in what we call the "astral body," which envelops the "spirit body." Souls remain inside this astral body for a certain period after death as they live in the Posthumous Realm of the fourth dimension. This astral body gives off vibrations that link the spirit world and Earth, so those in the fourth dimension generally live in this form.

When souls move up from the fourth dimension to a higher realm, they slough off their astral body because as long as they are wearing this kind of spiritual clothing, they will not be able to move on up to the true spirit world of the fifth dimension and beyond.

These astral bodies can be likened to thick diving suits; they are a little uncomfortable to wear, but necessary when diving down into the depths. Similarly, in a place with a vibration close to that of Earth, it is impossible to live without this kind of aid. Souls cannot move on to a higher plane while wearing it, however, so when they move up, they have to slough it off.

This astral body can be reused to create various phenomena in the Posthumous Realm or reused by spirits from higher realms when they come down to visit Earth. It is also used as the basic material for the rebirth of a soul.

Once the astral body has been cast off, there is the spirit body, which exists beneath the astral body. It is a little more refined than the astral body. Souls live in this form in the fifth dimension and above.

As souls move even higher and enter the realm of the Angels of Light, they find that even this spirit body feels extremely heavy, like wearing a suit of armor, so it becomes necessary to remove yet another layer, to become an even more refined "light body," which is filled with a fair degree of light. They move on to live in the sixth dimension and beyond in this light body.

The worlds that exist beyond the sixth dimension have subtler vibrations and are more refined. Therefore it is extremely hard for those in the seventh, eighth, or higher dimensions to come down to Earth and communicate with the people in this world. They become unable to communicate directly with people on Earth while they are in their true form.

Seen from the heavenly realm, even the astral body feels like a diving suit, so the physical bodies of people on Earth appear like iron armor. In this way, humans and high spirits emit completely different vibrations. To the inhabitants of the higher realms of the spirit world, humans appear like crabs with heavy shells lumbering across the bottom of the deep ocean. For this reason, it is extremely hard for them to be born on Earth in a physical body, or if they are not being born, even to send messages or offer guidance to people on Earth.

It is easier for evil spirits than high spirits To enter people on Earth

If you read books of spiritual messages, you may find that, in some cases, an intermediary takes part in them. A spirit from a lower realm appears and acts as a sort of medium in the spirit world, translating the words of the high spirit and passing on the messages to the people on Earth.

Sometimes a high spirit transmits messages through a young woman in her teens by automatic writing. In these cases, too, it is quite difficult for a high spirit to enter the girl directly so, in general, her guardian spirit acts as mediator. The high spirit makes her guardian spirit write or speak the messages. This kind of indirect sending of messages through a guardian spirit is very common.

If it were not done this way, the person on Earth receiving the message would not be able to bear the intense light of the spirit world. Moreover, as their vibrations do not match, it would be difficult for the high spirit to take complete control of the person's body. In this world, it is easier for a spirit from a neighboring realm to take over a human body completely.

When people in this world are living with a mind that is harmonized, it is, of course, difficult for spirits from Hell to approach them. In reality, however, many people are often driven by disharmonious thoughts such as anger, envy, hate, worry, pain, distress, and other such feelings. Sometimes, people's bodies are out of harmony because of illness or stress. If their work is hard, exhaustion can build up in the body, creating strain and causing problems with the heart, veins, organs, or brain, resulting in a physical breakdown. As minds and bodies sicken in this way, modern people emit vibrations closer to those of the lost spirits that lurk in the vicinity of Earth than to those of angels, and they are more susceptible to possession.

When your mind becomes fixed in a certain direction and your interests and likings match those of hellish spirits, then these spirits will sneak into your mind, moving in and out of your body. They may eventually settle in and take absolute control. Once this happens, even though your soul is still connected to the body by the "silver cord," your soul will be driven out of the body as another spirit takes it over, controlling it throughout your daily life.

There are a surprising number of people who find themselves in this sort of situation. They become a kind of "psychic medium," who specializes in evil spirits. These people usually suffer from severe mood swings and are unable to control their emotions. They are no longer themselves; their bodies are taken over by evil spirits.

In this world, there are many stray spirits who are unable to return to Heaven. In addition, there is a realm of Hell that very closely reflects the materialistic conditions of Earth. It is created by the thought energy of delusions and desires aroused in this world. The inhabitants of Hell tune in to the minds of people who emit this thought energy of desire. Therefore, if people open the spiritual doors in their minds, it is much easier for evil spirits from Hell to enter.

For example, if you are constantly drunk and your life is a shambles, then evil spirits will be able to enter your mind at will. I am sure that you have seen drunkards who are possessed by spirits and who have become unhinged. There are also those who are possessed and have gone insane, and are locked up in mental hospitals. These people have virtually become the equivalent of "psychics."

When an angel enters a person, that person's actions will not be strange, but if people are possessed by a lost soul from Hell or by the soul of somebody who committed suicide, then their actions will become abnormal. So most often, these people will be isolated from society. In reality, this kind of spiritual phenomenon happens.

Recently, we have been hearing about multiple personality disorders, but many of these cases are actually caused by evil spirits. When a spirit takes possession of a person, it drives out his or her soul, so the person will seem to take on a completely different personality. A possessing spirit cannot retain control forever, however, so when it tires, it leaves, and the body will be taken over by yet another spirit. In this way, five or ten spirits can interchangeably take over a person's body.

This is how many cases of multiple personality disorder are caused by possession. Sometimes a person's guardian spirit takes over the body, but, in most cases, the person's spiritual energy has become very weak, allowing other spirits to take over. The body becomes like an empty house and different spirits move in and out, creating a multiple personality disorder. This is a psychological state that is quite common among criminals.

In the case of spirits from higher realms, it is extremely difficult for them to communicate directly with a person on Earth due to the great difference in vibrations.

4

The Meaning of Religious Seclusion

Concentration of the mind is
A traditional method of attuning to the Spirit World

So then, what is the way to attune yourself to the spirit world? There is a traditional method that has been used since ancient times. The answer to this question is "concentration of the mind." Actually, all religions, both Eastern and Western, have their own methods of concentrating the mind.

Having said this, however, it is impossible to attune yourself perfectly because in certain circumstances, work and life in this world will stand in your way. The very fact that you are living in this world hinders your complete attunement to the spirit world. Even Swedenborg, who possessed a great spiritual power, had this trouble.

To visit the spirit world is, in some respects, the same as dying. When you travel to the other world while you are still living in this world, you will appear dead for two or three days and, during that time, you will not need to eat anything. To a layman, it will appear as if you have died, so there is a danger that your body may be disposed of while your soul is away. Therefore, while you are visiting the spirit world, it is important that you are left alone. As long as other people know what is going on and leave the body alone, it will be all right, but if they panic, and take the body to the hospital or hold a funeral, it will cause trouble.

For this reason, when Swedenborg went on one of his astral journeys, he would say to those around him, "Even though I appear dead, do not try to talk to me or touch me." In other words, he was saying that he could not contact the inhabitants of the other world unless he was in a state similar to death, and this is quite true. He also said, "If you have seen the spirit of a dead person, it means that you were also dead at that time," and, in a certain sense, this is also true.

In Buddhist scriptures, there are stories about how Buddha often went into seclusion for three months a year. As one of his habits, he generally did this in summer or in the rainy season. During this period, he shut out all contact with the outside world. For the rest of the year, he lived in monasteries with other disciples, gave sermons, and met people. He led a normal life and sometimes gave advice about the secular matters to the Sangha, but when he went on retreat, he cut himself off completely.

When a wealthy lay follower offered to provide Buddha with food for the summer, he would enter a cave or some similar place nearby and stay there. He had food delivered, but apart from that he had no contact with the outside world. He did not even go out to accept alms. Spending several months on retreat, isolated from the world, he would be detached from this world and would no longer be disturbed by the affairs of this world. If mundane matters intruded, he was unable to enter into deep meditation and spend a long time in the spirit world, so he went into seclusion.

In one of the scriptures, it is written that, during these three months, he returned to the heavenly realm where he preached to his mother, Mahamaya. He visited his mother, who had died when he was a baby, and taught her about the enlightenment that he had gained as Buddha.

Religious seclusion needs to last for long periods of time, otherwise you will not be able to attain a level where you can travel to and come back from the spirit world at will. In the present day, where you are always being interrupted by telephone calls, e-mails, faxes, and so on, where people come to visit you or where there are many noises that disturb your concentration, it is very difficult to communicate with the spirit world. Therefore it becomes necessary to cut yourself off from worldly matters.

Religious seclusion and missionary work
Are complementary aspects of religion

Although it appears paradoxical, in order to save many people in this world, you must cut yourself off from them. If you are unable to do this, you will not be able to save them.

This was true also of Jesus Christ. People at that time would idolize him, begging him in crowds to save them. Thousands would gather around him, but when his spiritual energy became low, he would escape from the crowds. He would flee by boat or seclude himself in the mountains where he could be alone.

If he did not retreat to some quiet place and be alone, he would not be able to recharge his spiritual energy; it was impossible for him to do this while he was in the midst of a noisy crowd. So he would go to a quiet place to meditate, recharge his spiritual energy, and wait until his strength returned. Once he became strong again, he was able to stand before the crowds and preach. At that time, he would become like a different person, overflowing with strength.

In this way, in religions, people follow a style of discipline wherein they supply themselves with spiritual energy, then expend it. The more light you expend, for instance through missionary work, the more important it becomes to live a meditative life and recharge yourself with light. For this reason, leaders of religions often retreat from the public eye to a quiet place in the mountains or forests. This is extremely important, and if you do not cleanse yourself of the dust and grime of your worldly life, you will be unable to continue your religious work.

As long as you live in this world, you cannot escape the mundane tasks of this world. You will have to devote a certain amount of time to the practical affairs of life, but as the time spent on this work increases, your spiritual qualities will gradually wane. On the contrary, however, if you spend all your time in meditation, then you will not be able to manage your mundane tasks and problems will occur in your work.

Religion is always a balance between these two conflicting aspects. Conversely, unless a religion contains these two conflicting facets, then it is not a real religion. If a religion is false, then it is possible to concentrate on just one facet. For example, a religion that does not have a spiritual side will be managed purely in a worldly manner.

On the other hand, there are religious people who concentrate solely on the spiritual side, such as hermits who spend all their time in retreat from the world. If they spend all their time meditating and training alone, however, then they will not be able to save people. They will not be able to offer salvation to others, but only for themselves.

There are surely many people who find happiness in such a lifestyle, but people who often go into retreat and concentrate only on saving themselves are the equivalent of hermits. Such people who become like hermits usually dislike organizations or crowds and, at the very most, they will only be able to create a small group of practitioners, similar to a social club.

Religious seclusion and large-scale missionary work are complementary aspects of religion. This is a theme that we at Happy Science too, have to continue working on to its completion.

In the past, before giving a lecture at a large venue, I would go into seclusion for a month or so. The longest period I spent in retreat was three months, cutting myself off from all contact with the outside world. When I am isolated in this way, however, various problems start to occur in the management of Happy Science and, as I work to solve them, the power I have built up through meditation drains away. This happened several times; I would recharge my spiritual power only to see it leak away and disappear.

As our organization continued to grow, whenever I went into seclusion, numerous problems would occur and damage our organization. This has made it increasingly difficult for me to be secluded from the matters of this world. This situation has continued for a long time now, and I have been unable to build up a large reservoir of energy.

In my case, I have the ability to receive spiritual messages or automatic writing continually on a daily basis. However, when it comes to automatic writing, writing down entire works from beginning to end in one sitting, without being distracted by any worldly thoughts, for instance, producing Happy Science's fundamental sutra, *Buddha's Teaching: The Dharma of the Right Mind*, has become extremely difficult. I can only go into this state once every five or ten years.

It is difficult to find the time to be secluded for a long period and my energy is constantly sapped by minor events. Receiving the most secret doctrines from the heavenly world is very difficult to do. While I am always capable of receiving messages from the spirit world, the earthly vibrations of the third dimension keep intruding and disturbing me, making it difficult to concentrate deeply.

In the beginning, I was able to produce whole books through automatic writing, but now it is much harder to do. I am unable to get away long enough to complete an entire book because there are all kinds of interruptions.

The growth of an organization is the realization of love in a tangible way in this world and is therefore necessary, but, simultaneously, it produces various problems in its management. So for leaders of religion, a growing organization could be a risk because it hinders them from recharging spiritually. An increasing number of worldly problems cause interference in the "direct line" to the realms of the higher spirits and can even result in crossed lines.

Communication with high spirits is impossible When surrounded by evil spirits

There are many cases where psychics start losing their ability to communicate with high spirits, although they were able to do so at the beginning. The Realm of Hell exists in close proximity to this world, so when psychics hold séances, evil spirits are generally attempting to prey on them, hoping to interfere.

How can evil spirits interfere with them? One way is to wait until psychics become exhausted. When psychics have used up all their spiritual power, they will become weak and so evil spirits can sneak into them.

Another way is for ten, twenty, or thirty evil spirits to come around the psychic, very much like a rugby scrum, building multiple walls around him or her. Once this happens, the psychic is no longer able to receive messages from his or her guardian spirit or high spirits.

The psychic is surrounded so densely by evil spirits that he or she becomes completely disconnected from the high spirits.

On such occasions, if the psychic cannot stop communicating with spirits for some reason, for example if he is a professional psychic and has been doing it for a living, he will then start telling people the words of evil spirits. In the majority of cases, this happens when the psychic is troubled by worldly matters. When he is unable to solve mundane problems, when he is worrying about something, or when he is filled with worldly desires, he is in most danger.

When evil spirits create a scrum around a psychic in this way, angels can only look on helplessly from a distance and, in many cases, they are unable to help. For this reason, there are many new religious groups that were good in the beginning, but at some point were taken over by evil spirits. You need to know that there is a power that targets religions to prevent them from carrying out their work.

Demonstrating spiritual phenomena
Consumes a great deal of energy

In the early stages of the Happy Science movement, I recorded large numbers of spiritual messages, but two hours was the limit for each session. After two hours, not only would my spiritual power be greatly diminished, but also Satan and other devils would begin to come close to disturb me. They knew that I was communicating with the high spirits and would try somehow to stop me. If I did not have the energy to repel them, they would stick around because they were so determined to stand in my way.

When my spiritual power was depleted, if I was not careful, devils would interfere, impersonating the voices of the high spirits and start giving me false messages. The spiritual lines would become crossed and the false messages would be mixed. It is very difficult to control one's physical condition, so two hours was the limit for one sitting.

Nevertheless, giving two hours of continuous spiritual messages is already quite tough and normal psychics would writhe on the ground in the agony of an extreme lack of energy. In the first part of this chapter, I spoke about using ectoplasm to create a body for ghosts. Just like that, it requires vast amounts of energy to create spiritual phenomena in this world.

I also described earlier how a spirit is covered by an "astral body," but, to be more precise, there is another subtle spirit body that exists between the physical body you have on Earth and the astral body you continue to use in the Posthumous Realm.

This subtle layer produces a faint electrical reaction around the body and forms a kind of biomagnetic energy. It is like an aura, and it differs from the astral body. It is difficult to describe, but there is a kind of etheric body that exists where the astral and physical bodies join.

When you perform a spiritual phenomenon, this part of your body becomes exhausted. Of course, you also use part of the astral body, but the etheric body is the main spiritual material that is used when creating spiritual phenomena.

For this reason, when communicating with the spirit world and conducting spiritual phenomena or receiving messages, a psychic, in most cases, creates a "circle" with people who always support him. It is a group of several or up to ten cooperative people, who believe in spiritual phenomena and who offer support by sending out thoughts of love.

When receiving spiritual messages, if the psychic relies on his own strength alone, he will soon become exhausted. But if there is this circle, energy flows toward him from these people, like strings of silk. The psychic demonstrates various spiritual phenomena while using these people's energy. Otherwise, if the psychic had to do this alone, he would run out of spiritual energy. One person's energy is soon exhausted, so a certain number of people need to be present to assist in creating spiritual phenomena.

If somebody present at a séance is a nonbeliever, doubting the truth of spiritual phenomena and intending to interrupt the proceedings, then the wavelength of the group is disturbed and spirits are unable to descend. If disruptive thoughts enter the group, then the psychic will be unable to gather sufficient energy and fail to call down spirits. If a materialist or quack scientist enters the group, it will cause confusion and generally make it impossible to call down spirits.

These people come with the sole aim of obstructing the proceedings and then when the psychic is unable to create the phenomenon, they will be the first to proclaim the séance a fake and fraud. This is a common occurrence. Therefore, when a psychic tries to communicate with a spirit, he needs to have people around him who will supply him with energy, otherwise it will be very difficult to transform the energy of the higher spirits into energy of this world and emit it. This is how spiritual phenomena occur.

In Happy Science, members devote themselves to the outward activities of religion such as missionary work, but when it comes to defending our organization, I feel that we are still lacking in strength. There are some areas that need to be defended systematically, but not everyone is fully able to understand the importance of religious seclusion. Even our renunciant disciples have various mundane tasks to do and so they are probably unable to take time to devote themselves to meditation or spiritual practices.

It is a fact that the ability to communicate with high spirits is an innate ability, but the ability to receive guidance from your personal guardian spirit is something that can be achieved in life through personal effort. Those active in religions have work to do in this world, however, and are usually very busy. Particularly if they have children to raise, they will have very little chance to escape from secular life. Schoolteachers, tutors, neighbors, and friends may call on them at times and it is impossible to cut off completely all relationships with people in this world.

This is why, in the past, many seekers of the truth were unmarried. Unmarried people could easily cut themselves off from society, but it is not so easy for people with a family. They are unable to break away from society or live apart from others. Therefore it is difficult to find the time for religious seclusion.

5
Balancing Spiritual Ability
With Work Ability

Before starting spiritual training,
Worldly ability is necessary

When it comes to spiritual training, it is not a good idea to go into religious seclusion and meditate right away. Even if you concentrate on practicing meditation from the very start of your spiritual training, in most cases it would be a waste of time.

In Christianity as well as Buddhism, monks and nuns are first assigned daily chores and mundane work to do. Only after they prove their worldly ability are they allowed to start their spiritual training. Otherwise, the effort of their spiritual training is wasted.

No matter how hard people with little ability to perform worldly tasks work to accumulate spiritual training, it is the equivalent of trying to make an empty sack stand on its own. A sack will not stand unless there is something in it. Therefore you must first check if you have a certain degree of leadership ability, insight, intellect not deluded by evil spirits, and confidence at having built yourself up in the past.

People who do not have these characteristics will be overcome by evil spirits or the devil. If they have not disciplined themselves extensively enough, they will be prone to conceit, leaving themselves open to attack, and their body will soon be taken over by evil spirits. This is likely to happen because in this world, evil spirits are much more common than high spirits.

People who have not undergone stern self-discipline, who do not keep making efforts humbly, who do not have a certain degree of insight or the ability to discriminate at work, will soon believe the tempting words of evil spirits, which they can hear while undergoing spiritual life. They will not realize that what they hear is wrong. For this reason, it is vital that you have enough intelligence and experience of this world to be able to discern and put a limit on what you hear from the spirits.

Paradoxically, however, the more intelligence and experience you gain in this world, the less spiritual you may become. This is the difficult part. The more able you become at secular tasks, the less spiritual you may become. Only a very low percentage of people are able to excel in both fields.

When receiving various messages from high spirits, it is better for mediums to be well educated because this will provide them with a greater vocabulary and power of expression, allowing them to transmit more information. However, it is quite common for well-educated people to find it difficult to believe in spiritual matters. Their knowledge and learning stand in the way of believing; they lose their open-mindedness and become incapable of receiving messages from spirits. In this respect, it can be most difficult to balance the two.

It takes great discipline to be able to study well, possess knowledge, and be good at one's job while remaining open-hearted, humble, always reflecting on oneself, and ready to receive messages from higher dimensions with a selfless heart. It is necessary to be able to balance these paradoxical aspects, but there are very few people who are capable of achieving this.

Balancing the spiritual and the worldly

One way to solve this issue, although it is a compromise, is to assign someone who has an understanding of spiritual things and at the same time is good at managing earthly affairs to work as a team with a pure and spiritual person. This method is used by the majority of religions.

Some people are knowledgeable about the management of earthly affairs and also sympathetic to religion. If they know very well that they cannot achieve the heights of spirituality but are content to be supporting a spiritual person from a worldly perspective, they can be teamed up with somebody who can delve deeply into the spiritual world but who does not understand earthly matters and is likely to find themselves in trouble without somebody's protection.

If the power of these two people is well balanced, they will be able to create a good religious group and develop it, but if the balance is lost, then their religion will become misguided. If the organization becomes too spiritual, it will start performing strange rituals as a group, and if it becomes too earthly, its religious activities will become businesslike. Achieving this balance is extremely important. It is difficult to sustain a religious organization unless people within it strive to bring out their strengths while compensating for weaknesses.

In general, business ability requires a kind of psychokinetic power in the sense that you actively give out your willpower toward creating or accomplishing something. The same could also be said of debating ability. On the other hand, spiritual ability mainly requires a receptive power, so you need to be extremely passive. It is the ability to be quiet, passive, and receptive.

It is hard for an active nature to be compatible with a passive nature. An active person rarely receives inspiration, while a passive person often does but tends not to take action. It is very difficult to switch between these two abilities. One cannot receive inspiration without being passive, but a passive person often appears to be incapable of doing a secular job and appears quite inept. Switching between these two is difficult, so it is important that you know which quality is stronger in you, know your limits, and cooperate accordingly with other people.

Without having an active side, it will be impossible for an organization to grow large. The ability to push and spread the teachings is vital, but, at its core, a religion must also have the ability to be passive and be able to receive inspiration.

I sometimes need to go into retreat and receive light, but this is true for all renunciant disciples of Happy Science. You need to create an environment in which you can receive light from your guardian and guiding spirits. If you preach or conduct religious ceremonies without recharging spiritually, your mind will be filled with busy thoughts and the various emotions of this world. Then you will only be emitting rough "beta wavelengths." If you do not emit "alpha wavelengths" or meditative wavelengths, you will be unable to receive spiritual guidance or energy.

"Beta wavelengths" are the wavelengths that you often emit while doing a job in this world. These waves are emitted from your mind when you are working amidst many telephone calls, exchanging documents, and holding meetings. In this sort of environment, it is impossible for high spirits to come down. The only spirits that are capable of descending in these conditions are the spirits with strong psychokinetic power. As I wrote earlier, spirits living close to Earth are good at creating physical phenomena and these spirits with a psychokinetic power are able to come while you are quite active, but the spirits who send revelatory messages usually cannot.

Therefore, to receive spiritual messages, "relaxation," "peace of mind," "tranquility," and "silence" are extremely necessary. It is important to understand that, in a religion, both the active and passive sides are required in a systematic way.

6

Religion Has Two Main Tasks: To Recharge Spiritual Energy and Promote Missionary Work

In this chapter, I have dealt with the subject "the Principle of Channeling." I would like you all to know that religion has two main tasks: recharging spiritual energy and promoting missionary work. One is the work of recharging spiritual energy, the task of receiving spiritual messages and light, while the other is translating this light into earthly forms and spreading it around. It is insufficient to do just one of these. Both are necessary.

If possible, it is good to divide your time and choose different places to experience each one. But if you feel that you have an innate aptitude for only one of these abilities, then focus on your strength while leaving the weaker side to somebody who excels at it. It is important that you think in this way and create this style.

If a religion carries out only one of these tasks, it will eventually collapse, so both of these are necessary. The more a religion grows and expands externally, the greater the energy it needs internally through religious seclusion. For instance, at Happy Science, as the local branches become more and more active in spreading the teachings far and wide, at the same time, we must also have many opportunities to undergo religious training, recharge ourselves spiritually, and practice meditation in staff seminars in temples or *shojas*.

It is impossible to enlarge only externally without developing internally. If a religion tries to grow only outwardly, then it will be no different from a company. Conversely, if a religion only grows internally, without carrying out missionary work, then it will not be able to fulfill its mission here on Earth. If people hardly influence the outside world and spend all their time in retreat, then their endeavor will go to waste. Therefore both tasks are necessary.

It is not possible to do earthly work while maintaining alpha waves. Most people who are good at working emit beta waves. So when do you emit alpha waves? When you write a poem, for instance, you wait passively for the right words to spring to mind. You remain open, choosing the words you need; that is when your mind is close to the alpha state. Conversely, when you are on the telephone, negotiating with customers, then you are in beta mode. While it is important to be praised for being good at work in this world, this has nothing to do with conducting spiritual work.

When you are in beta mode, high spirits cannot send messages directly to you. At the very best, you can only communicate with them through spiritual beings who exist in the realms near Earth and have them pass on the messages indirectly. Moreover, when your mind becomes too accustomed to the beta mode, you will leave yourself open to possession by evil spirits and they will stay with you, so you need to be careful.

This is the principle by which religions operate. They are quite different from businesses or companies. Businesspeople will usually be in alpha mode on the weekend, after returning home, or when they are enjoying leisure, travel, or a walk, but in a religion, maintaining a meditative state and being in alpha mode is also important work. Talking with other people and solving various earthly problems is equally important. Please understand that the work of a religion is incomplete unless it is capable of encompassing both of these contradictory elements.

Note: Recently, in addition to "alpha waves," people have started to categorize some waves as "theta waves" and "delta waves." I agree with these notions, as there is a slight difference between alpha waves [relaxing mode], theta waves [drowsy mode], and delta waves [the state of deep sleep].

Chapter Four

Occultism as Power

~ Release the Power Bound by
The Commonly Accepted Knowledge ~

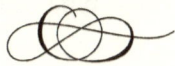

Lecture given on December 10, 2000

1
What Is Occultism?

The original meaning of occult—*something hidden*

In this chapter, I will venture to talk on the subject of the occult. Today, the word *occult* conjures up images of grotesque spiritual phenomena and frightening ghost tales, but here I am going to talk on the subject of the occult from a religious perspective, and I will not use the word "occult" in that type of negative context.

In today's terminology, occultism has a meaning that is similar to mysticism or mystical thought, but, essentially, occultism originally meant "something hidden" or "concealed." The word "occult" has a very deep meaning because here are to be found the secrets of religion and the secrets of Buddha or God, the object of religious faith. These are basically hidden or kept secret.

Why is it that these truths have been kept secret?

When I think about this, I realize that many of these secrets have already been revealed in my movie, *The Laws of the Sun* [executive producer Ryuho Okawa, released October 2000]. I think most people who have been raised and educated in today's society will be surprised when they watch this movie or read the original book, *The Laws of the Sun* [published by IRH Press]. This movie and book contain truths they have never learned or studied anywhere before.

Actually, there are many truths that people do not know because there is nowhere they can learn about them. They do not possess even a basic foundation of knowledge to understand them. This is not merely because they have not obtained the necessary knowledge, however; some of it has been kept secret. Why is this? It is a philosophical issue to find out why such knowledge has been kept hidden, or a more impressive religious theme that transcends philosophy.

This world is isolated from the true world

All beings in this world live under certain rules. Let us say that you keep goldfish in an aquarium filled with water. The aquarium has aquatic plants and gravel on the bottom. The fish swim around inside the tank and live off the food that they are fed. The world we live in is very much like this aquarium. Just like the tank, this world is a limited world and is governed by certain rules. The fish in the tank are constrained to follow these rules; these rules are unchangeable.

As the fish swim through the water, they come to a glass side and are unable to go any farther. Even if they swim to the left, the right, or backward, they find there are other glass walls to block them. Below them is the floor of the aquarium, much like the ground here on Earth, and no matter how hard they may try, they are unable to break out that way. An aquarium has a set size, and it is impossible to leave; there are physical boundaries that cannot be overcome. Of course, the top is open, but the fish are incapable of flying, and anyway, they know that they cannot live out of water.

All they have in their world is a floor covered with small white stones, some plants, a mysterious supply of food, and the other fish they spend their entire lives with. If they talk to the other fish, the others will say, "Our world here inside the aquarium is the only real world. We know nothing about the world outside." They have no idea of what might exist beyond their world, and they do not have enough courage to go out and explore.

Even if one of the fish claims to have jumped into the air and seen the outside world, the other fish cannot believe it. "You only had a glimpse of it when you jumped," they will say. "Nobody has ever explored the world outside and come back alive to tell us about it." They may well say this and it is difficult to deny it when they are actually living inside the aquarium. For the goldfish, the world outside their aquarium is unreal—it is a world of the imagination. Life in the three-dimensional earthly world is very similar to this.

Suppose one of the fish were suddenly to sprout wings and became able to leave the aquarium. If the winged fish were to fly around exploring the outside world and return to tell the others what he had seen, what would they say? Most likely, the other fish would refuse to believe what he had to say, they would criticize or ignore him. I think that this is very similar to the situation of religion today.

Then again, if all the fish wanted to explore the truth and jumped out of the aquarium, would they become happy and understand the truth? I'm afraid not. If they were all to jump out of the aquarium, they would no longer be able to come back. The world that surrounds the tank is vast and boundless; it is the true world. Fish cannot live outside the aquarium, however, and they must swim around in the heavy water. This is the absolute condition that governs their lives.

This is exactly the situation that humans are in. So there is a reason why people do not want to hear about the true world. They are unable to understand it, because the world they live in is so different from the true world.

If the goldfish tried to become inhabitants of the outside world, they would die. The fish will only learn of the outside world when their lives have ended. If they are ready to die, they will be able to visit the outside world; once they accept their death, they can go out of the aquarium.

It would be terrible, however, if humans had to die to understand the true world. That is why there are certain exceptions and, just like the flying goldfish, someone with special abilities appears, visits the other world, and returns to tell others about it, while other people half believe what is shared.

After a certain time, another person appears and again tells people about the true world. In this way, knowledge about the true world, the seed of truth, always remains in this world. Throughout history, this kind of person has always appeared at regular intervals to teach others about the true world. The people listen, half believing, but certainly they ponder it. This is the situation that has continued.

So why should the existence of the spirit world be hidden from people? Because when people are able to understand it completely, they no longer belong to this world. This hidden truth is only made obvious when people die. Living in this world is the same as living inside an aquarium; we are living in a place that is cut off from the true world.

The reason people are born into this world

Some people may ask why this world was separated from the other world in the first place, but if you look at it from the perspective of the spirit world, you will understand the reason. Actually, this world is a very good place to learn lessons for soul training.

The spirit world is a world of complete freedom, but if you are living there, it is hard to appreciate this spiritual freedom. It is only when you have been born on Earth that you can understand the value of this spiritual freedom. For that reason, despite all the pain it involves, you will choose to be reborn on Earth time and again.

There are people who like running marathons, despite the rigor this involves, as well as people who like to swim, despite the exertion. They continue practicing because they wish to test their abilities within a given set of rules.

Running twenty-six miles in a marathon, swimming, or practicing judo are all hard on the body, but people do not stop doing them. Why is this? It is because they wish to overcome any handicaps and test the limits of their abilities. They wish to better themselves and win the respect of others.

For the same reason, people are born into this world, this particular world. This system may appear strange, but the fact that our lifespan in this world is limited shows that God or Buddha has not set it up with an intention to punish us or make us suffer. It would be very mean of God or Buddha if we were sent to live on Earth forever when there is a world of freedom in the spirit world. But our time on Earth is limited.

Humans can live up to about one hundred years, while animals live a much shorter span than that. Insects live an even shorter time, mostly less than one year. Since you are only here for a limited time, you cannot understand all the truths of the world, and because you do not understand everything, you will make efforts to get to know them. As you live spiritually blind, you may go through numerous hardships, but it will give you a store of experience and strengthen your soul. It is similar to climbing a mountain; you choose to undergo difficulties and train your soul.

This is the standpoint that you should adopt when you think about mysticism or occultism. From the perspective of this material world, the spirit world may seem a peculiar place that only a small number of people believe in. It is a world that is a bit scary and off-putting, but from another perspective, the spirit world is the true world, while this world is quite peculiar.

In this world, it is impossible to live without oxygen; you will die within a few minutes. In the spirit world, however, oxygen is no longer necessary. You will not die even without oxygen. In this world, you cannot live without eating, but in the other world, you will not die even if you never eat. The world we are living in right now is like an aquarium and humans on Earth are the equivalent of goldfish living in an aquarium. We live in such a special world.

Therefore, although you may now be living according to the rules of this world, you must not completely forget about the original spirit world. That is why we need continually to inform people about the world beyond, the open world. My soul group is closely involved in this work.

2

The History of Western Occultism

"Thoth-Hermes" of Ancient Egypt

The origin of Western occultism can be traced back to ancient Egypt or Greece. In Egypt, people often talk of "Hermes Trismegistus" [thrice greatest Hermes] or "Thoth-Hermes." Thoth and Hermes are different people, but in Egyptian mythology, the two are treated as a single being and, without knowing the reason for this, the myth has been passed down to the present day.

Actually, Thoth-Hermes means that Thoth and Hermes are one and the same. Unless you learn about the system of soul siblings, however, you will not be able to understand why Thoth and Hermes are one being. As taught at Happy Science, Thoth was born in Atlantis while Hermes was born in Greece. In short, Hermes is the reincarnation of Thoth, and they belong to the same soul group.

Thoth from Atlantis came to be widely known in Egypt as the god Thoth, revered as the god of wisdom, learning, technology, and art. Thoth is said to have invented academic study and to have created special words and various forms of art.

Modern Egyptology calculates that the Egyptian pyramids and the sphinx were created approximately three to five thousand years ago, that is to say, between one and three thousand years B.C. As a result, Egyptologists believe that ancient civilizations existed in Egypt approximately five thousand years ago, and they are doubtful about any civilizations before that time.

However, the fact that Thoth, who was a real person, is now regarded as a mythological god shows how long ago he existed. If he had been a man who lived four or five thousand years ago, then he would not have been called a god. People who lived three or four thousand years ago are still known today by their real names, such as the Pharaoh Khafra or Amenhotep IV [Akhenaten]. If Thoth had lived at the same time as these kings, then he would not have been regarded as a god. The fact that he was listed among the mythological gods indicates that he lived much earlier.

Although archeologists remain unconvinced, well-known researchers with an occult bent recently reported that the sphinx and some of the pyramids date back over ten thousand years, which would mean that they were built at around the same time that the continent of Atlantis disappeared below the sea.* As proof, the sphinx is said to shows signs of water erosion caused by massive rainfall. Today the sphinx stands in a desert and, although it would make sense that it had been eroded by wind, the traces point unmistakably to rain. This would be impossible in Egypt as it is today and can only mean that it has stood there since a time when the country had a warm, moist climate.

So when could this have been? The Ice Age continued up until a little over ten thousand years ago and, for a period of several thousand years after that, there was a warm temperate climate until another climatic change, which resulted in Egypt being turned into a desert. This means that the sphinx must have been built during the temperate period, which makes it more than five thousand years old. At the very least, the erosion must have taken place between five and seven thousand years ago and so it must have been constructed even earlier than that. It can probably be dated as somewhere between seven and ten thousand years old.†

As I have written in *The Laws of the Sun*, there were also pyramids in Mu and Atlantis. There were people who constructed pyramids in that period and their

---

* Refer to Graham Hancock, *Fingerprints of the Gods* (New York, Crown Publishing).

†Refer to Robert M. Schoch and Robert Aquinas McNally, *Voices of the Rocks*; John Anthony West, *Serpent in the Sky*.

philosophy was handed down to the Egyptians. While the pyramids in Egypt are made of huge stones, in the times of Mu and Atlantis, people created pyramids out of materials other than stone. The pyramids in Egypt are indeed the result of a passing down of the philosophy of the pyramids in Atlantis.

Egyptians believe that the god of wisdom in Egypt is the god Thoth and all the wisdom that existed in Egypt has come from Thoth. In fact, Thoth is a god from Atlantis, and this Thoth was combined with Hermes to become known as "Hermes Trismegistus." Thus the philosophy of Hermes in Greece was combined with the philosophy of Thoth in Atlantis, producing the philosophy of Ancient Egypt.

Hermes' philosophy is the origin of Western philosophy

Prior to Christianity, religious thought prevailed in Ancient Egypt, and people built pyramids and believed in reincarnation. They believed that the dead would return to life, so, in preparation for their resurrection, they created mummies, put adornments in the graves, and built houses for the dead.

Ancient Egyptians also believed strongly that Egypt on Earth was a projection of the heavenly realm in the spirit world. To them, the existence of the other world was irrefutable fact, and they clearly understood that humans transmigrated between this world and the next. This philosophy of the spirit world actually came from Hermes and has been passed down to the present day under the name "Hermetica."

Hermes' philosophy had an extremely powerful influence on Christianity, and much Christian ideology has its roots in Egyptian thinking. Christianity goes to great lengths to emphasize that Christ was resurrected after dying on the cross, and although this concept of resurrection appears to be highly original, it is merely a throwback to Egyptian philosophy in which the dead were all resurrected.

The Egyptians believed that the dead would be resurrected and therefore they preserved people's bodies after death in the form of mummies. Their image of resurrection was not quite accurate, however. While mummies may stand as symbols of resurrection, they never actually came back to life. The truth was that the souls of the dead are resurrected in the other world and then eventually reincarnate in this world.

In this way, Egyptian thinking was incorporated into Christianity to become one of its underlying concepts. The philosophy of Thoth was combined with that of Hermes from several thousand years ago, gained more strength, and went on to become the philosophy of Egypt, of Israel, and, eventually, of modern Europe.

The philosophy of Hermes, which taught the secret doctrines of the spirit world, became the mysticism of ancient Egypt and was then incorporated into Islam. Much of Hermes' philosophy was incorporated into Islam where it forms an undercurrent of mysticism. It is the same philosophy that influenced Christianity.

This philosophy of Hermes also flowed into Europe. Many mystic philosophies existed in Europe and these continued to exist even after the Middle Ages. Even today we hear about the ancient and mystical order Rosae Crucis [the Rosicrucian Order] or the Freemasons, and these secret societies are based on the ancient philosophies of Hermes, the mysticism of the spirit world. In this way, the philosophy of Hermes forms the origin of Western thought.

Hermes' philosophy —
The foundation of modern science

Hermes' philosophy has not only affected religion, but has also formed the foundation of modern science. Hermes taught heliocentricism, which states that the sun is the center of the universe and all planets circle around the sun. To be more accurate, this concept has been passed down as the Thoth-Hermes philosophy and has been known since before the birth of Christ.

In the field of empirical science, it was believed for a long time that the Earth was the center of the universe and all the planets circled around it. Most astronomers in the past supported the Ptolemaic theory and believed that the Earth was at the center. It was only much later that Nicolaus Copernicus [1473–1543] proposed that the Earth actually circled the sun, and Hermes' philosophy underlies his theory. Today the idea of heliocentricism is accepted as the truth, thanks to the efforts of numerous scientists over the years to prove this.

Isaac Newton [1643–1727] was another scientist whose ideas were strongly influenced by the philosophy of Hermes. In the modern era, William Harvey [1578–1657] developed the theory of the circulation of blood and, before that, Michael Servetus [1511–1553] came up with the theory of pulmonary circulation based on Hermes' concept of cyclical time.

Hermes' concept of cyclical time states that time progresses in a cyclic manner and it travels in a circular motion. In order to prove this concept, scientists used it as a basis for their work and came up with the theory of the circulation of blood. In this way, even modern science was influenced by the philosophy of the spirit world.

When we talk of the natural sciences, the first name that springs to mind is Aristotle. He is considered the father of natural science, which later blossomed to create the modern science that we know today. Although Aristotle devoted a lot of enthusiasm to logical proofs using words, however, he did not like to do mathematical proofs. As a result, although scientists may have adopted his philosophy, they could not contribute to the development of the natural sciences that are backed up by substantial mathematical proof, as we know today.

Actually, natural science based on mathematics finds its roots in the philosophy of Hermes. Hermes' philosophy was transmitted from Egypt to Greece where it had a strong influence on Pythagoras and other Greek mathematicians.

Hermes' philosophy can be classified as part of the occult, but it also has had a great influence on modern science and has some affinity with it. Although it may seem strange, Hermes' philosophy combines aspects of both the occult and science.

The same was also true of Atlantis. Although mysticism strongly influenced Atlantean society, Atlantis was also extremely advanced technologically. The same could be said of Mu; great advances were made when mysticism was dominant. Both civilizations shared these two aspects.

This duality was also the case with Shakyamuni Buddha. He taught about attaining enlightenment in the world of the mind and fighting against evil, which shows that he had mystical philosophies. But as well as being a mystic, he also possessed a rational mind that allowed him to handle secular issues effectively.

The duality of mysticism and rationalism is a characteristic of El Cantare. El Cantare has this duality because here we find a fundamental way of thinking with regard to the activities of all life on Earth. El Cantare wishes to make life on Earth a meaningful experience for humans, so He provides philosophies that are realistic and practical for life on Earth. However, to prevent people from being absorbed by worldly matters and completely denying the other world, El Cantare also provides something of the mystical or occult as an opposing value. That is why El Cantare expresses both of these facets in this world.

Spiritual abilities or supernatural phenomena are fundamentally supposed to be hidden, but displaying them occasionally serves to shake people's reason. When people become too enamored by reason, they think only of this world and so spiritual phenomena, miracles, or other mysterious incidents take place every now and again to shake their reason.

3
UFOs and the Science
Of the Spirit World

UFOs travel through the Spirit World

In recent years, sightings of UFOs have become quite common. UFOs have been coming to Earth since ancient times, but there has been a remarkable rise in sightings in modern times. This is because, ever since people on Earth have been able to fly, their outlook and perspective on the sky or space has changed. Things that would have been considered myths in olden times are now being understood as real. With regard to the issue of UFOs, Rient Arl Croud holds the key to interactions in outer space and is in charge of regulating alien immigration in the El Cantare Spirit Group.

There have been many reports of UFOs describing how they appear and disappear, or move around like ghosts. They are said to disappear and reappear at random, and flicker across the sky. A UFO can be picked up on radar when it is visible, but as soon as it disappears, it also vanishes from radar screens. It is a strange phenomenon. According to the laws of this world, if an object can be captured on radar, then it should remain there and, likewise, an object that does not register on radar should remain undetectable. A

UFO, however, will disappear and reappear physically and on radar.

UFOs operate in the three-dimensional world, so they are not entirely spiritual objects. They belong to beings who have a foothold here in the three-dimensional world. In fact, the inhabitants of other planets know how to travel through the spirit world. They use the route to travel between this world and the next; this shows the level their science has achieved.

Our science here on Earth is also approaching the same level, but we need to take one more theoretical step forward to gain the ability to travel between this world and the other. The problem is that the majority of scientists are still unable to believe that it is possible for objects of this world to become objects not of this world.

At the level of elementary particles, however, it is difficult to say whether they are material objects or not. As can be seen from the equation $E = mc^2$ [energy = mass $\times$ (the speed of light)^2], matter and energy can be converted to parity, which means that matter and energy are the equivalent of each other. Therefore, scientifically speaking, matter is energy and energy is matter.

Scientists have yet to grasp the full implications of this equation. They are unable to understand it because they only think of energy as being something belonging to this world. But if they apply this law to the spirit world as well, they should be able to understand that the light energy of the spirit world could materialize and be converted into matter in this world. In other words, energy could appear as matter in this world, and it could also disappear again. According to the law that runs through this world and the spirit world, it is true that energy and matter are interchangeable.

Unless scientists take the spirit world into account, it is hard for them to understand this theory. For instance, if somebody performed spoon bending and the spoon broke, a scientist would not believe it, saying that the disappearance of matter would create a massive explosion like an atom bomb, releasing vast amounts of energy. They think it is impossible for a part of the spoon to disappear without a massive release of energy. This may be true according to the science of this world, and that is why it is difficult for scientists to understand it. However, science must advance one more step to the next stage.

As science continues to explore and clarify the truth about space, UFOs, and aliens, I believe that the technology to transcend the boundary between this world and the spirit world will also be invented. I assume the large part of this truth will be uncovered during the twenty-first century. There are already beings who travel through the fourth dimension to visit Earth, so this must be the aim of study and research.

In the spirit world, distance does not exist.

Inhabitants may feel or imagine that there is a distance between places or objects, but the distance does not actually exist. Therefore, if one passed through the spirit world, it would be possible to travel from the Earth to the Moon, Mars, or even somewhere outside the Solar System or the Milky Way in the blink of an eye.

The straight-line distance between two places may be very long in this world, but if you travel through the fourth dimension or above, distances in this world are no longer what they seem to be. For instance, let us say a person enters a marathon and runs twenty-six miles in a straight line. The distance of twenty-six miles is an objective fact that cannot be changed. The only way to shorten the traveling time is to use a faster mode of transport, such as a bicycle, a car, or even a helicopter. That is why, today, scientists strive to produce faster vehicles, such as rockets, in order to shorten the travel time.

If scientists were to use the science of the spirit world, however, it would be possible to bend what appears to be a straight line and connect the two edges to create a circle. If they determine a destination spiritually, they can join the departure point and the destination, allowing them to travel anywhere in an instant. This is the way it is in the spirit world and, for this reason, its inhabitants do not share the three-dimensional concept of distance.

In order to travel through the spirit world, warp technology is necessary, as well as higher awareness to be able to understand and accept the spirit world. It would probably be quicker to obtain warp technology from aliens, but even if we do not, I am sure that we will eventually be able to develop our own technology to travel through other dimensions. Recent scientific theory claims that warp technology is impossible, but that is wrong; scientists must go beyond the three-dimensional perspective.

Aliens travel through other dimensions by spaceship to visit Earth. From their planets to Earth takes several light-years or tens of light-years, so if they were to travel through the third dimension, they would grow too old to return home, but by passing through other dimensions, they can travel instantaneously.

When a spaceship is passing through another dimension, the passengers also enter the other dimension and, although they may feel that their bodies have not changed, seen objectively, their bodies are in a completely different state. When a body from the world of matter travels through another dimension, it is "translated" into light energy. Not only the spaceship itself, but also the passengers are turned into mere energy. In other words, they are like souls or death candles. While passing through another dimension, aliens are transformed into energy bodies, but they probably recognize themselves as being the same.

In this way, aliens travel back and forth between planets. Even though we may not be able to acquire all of this scientific technology during the twenty-first century, I am sure that, to some extent, much will become clear about this mechanism.

Numerous species of aliens visit Earth

There are actually many different species of aliens who travel through other dimensions to visit Earth and it is difficult to know how many species have come here. The species most similar to humans on Earth resemble the Caucasian race; they have fair skin, blond or silver hair, and straight noses. They are very similar to humans on Earth and I think that their bodies have adapted in a way that is very close to human.

There are also reptile-type aliens as depicted in our movie, *The Laws of the Sun*. Others are the well-known Grey Aliens, which have almond-shaped eyes and are only about fifty inches tall. To be quite concise, however, Greys are not true living beings but have been created as a kind of cyborg.

There are also what are known as the "Bigfoot," a race of giant aliens. Their bodies are covered with hair, their feet are longer than twenty-four inches, and they are almost ten feet tall. They resemble a kind of yeti or abominable snowman. Actually, on their own planet, these are not the human race but are kept as pets. In earthly terms, they would be like dinosaurs that have devolved. Bigfoots were originally aggressive, combative animals, but since degenerating, they have been tamed and kept as pets.

Numerous species of aliens have visited Earth and they actually come and go. In Japan, however, information about these aliens is as scarce as information about the spirit world. It is considered only proper and true to doubt their existence. This country purposely cuts itself off from information and very little manages to get in. A certain amount of information does get transmitted, but it very rarely appears in the media, and when it does, it is generally presented as a hoax. Therefore, when it comes to knowledge about aliens, the Japanese remain quite uninformed.

The truth about UFO abductions

In the United States today, the number of encounters with UFOs and abductions by extraterrestrials has risen alarmingly, giving cause for worry.* In most cases, subjects have no recollection of the event because they have been hypnotized to forget everything.

---

* For further information, refer to John E. Mack's *Abduction: Human Encounters with Aliens* (Ballantine Books). The author is a professor of psychiatry at Harvard Medical School's Cambridge Hospital. The following information is based on this book.

There are many cases in which the subjects complain of nosebleeds and, when their noses are checked, small particles of metal are found embedded in them. When these people are put under regressive hypnosis, they talk about being abducted by UFOs, but they cannot consciously recall the events. There have been so many cases of this kind; large numbers of people have been abducted and it has become a serious problem.*

What happens when a person is abducted is always very similar, so it must be true. Even though we know it is true, however, there is such a gulf between the alien technologies and ours that nothing can be done about the abductions.

In most cases of alien abduction, the subject is in the bedroom or driving alone down the highway at night when they suddenly lose consciousness and, when they come around, they find that approximately an hour has passed. During that time, they have been taken up into a flying saucer, where their body has been studied or experimented upon. In the case of women, sometimes they have undergone experiments to create offspring that are half alien.

We know that aliens are doing these sorts of things, but they have been erased from people's memories. Only under hypnosis when they are regressed will they

---

* Refer to Colin Wilson, *Alien Dawn: An Investigation into the Contact Experience* (Fromm International).

learn that a UFO appeared, a bright light shone, and then an alien came out. In most cases, these aliens are Greys.

What is surprising is that aliens are able to abduct people through physical barriers such as walls. When an alien shines some kind of ray on a person, he or she will float in the air and pass through a closed window or door as if it did not exist. This phenomenon is similar to what happens when the soul leaves the body during an out-of-body experience. The nature of this tractor beam emitted from UFOs will certainly be examined and researched in the future.

The majority of UFO abductions seem to take place in the United States and I presume that the United States was chosen for their research because it is the most advanced country in the world. Moreover, if people were abducted in a crowded country like Japan, the UFOs would surely be seen, so they avoid highly populated countries. The United States is a large country with many isolated homes and empty highways so it would be much easier for them to work there unnoticed.

There is a huge technological gap between them and us, making it easy for them to abduct people on Earth and carry out various experiments. It is similar to the way that we capture and tag migratory birds or salmon fry to do research. So, although we know that these abductions are taking place, there is too great a gap in the technologies for us to be able to do anything to stop them.

Extraterrestrials are capable of moving between the third and fourth dimensions and they can even pass through solid walls, so we cannot capture and arrest them. It would be like trying to capture a ghost.

These kinds of phenomena often occur and I believe they will become a major challenge for us during the twenty-first century. We have been witnessing more and more UFO activity, especially in recent years, ever since humankind developed the technology to travel through the sky and reach out into the universe. This has stimulated the aliens to take a greater interest in us. In olden times, when humanity had very little knowledge of the universe, it would not have been exciting for aliens to interact with us, but now that humans on Earth have got to know more about the universe, they may find it interesting to provoke us in this way.

Looking at the actions of the aliens, however, there seems to be an element of mischief in what they do. It seems to me that young aliens are coming to Earth, enjoying teasing its inhabitants and conducting experiments that are similar to school science projects. A lot of what they do does not seem to be the work of adults but rather child's play. They seem to think that as long as they are not found out, they can do as they please.

Constraints on extraterrestrial intervention
In the affairs of Earth

As I have described so far, there are many mysterious phenomena in this world. I believe that Happy Science would not be able to accomplish its purpose if we were to deny this sort of occultism and mysticism.

The true recognition of this world is as follows: the three-dimensional realm is like the world inside an aquarium, and there is a vast and boundless world beyond its boundaries. The aquarium and the outside world are not completely separate, however; rather, the aquarium is contained within a vast, limitless world.

Those in the outside world are able to intervene freely in the world inside the aquarium, for example, putting their hands in, stirring it with a stick, or feeding its inhabitants. For example, humans outside the aquarium are able to put their hands in and catch one of the fish. The remaining fish are unable to understand what has happened, simply noticing that one of their numbers has disappeared. Some time later, however, the fish that disappeared is dropped back in from above and all the others are amazed at its sudden reappearance. The abductions by UFOs are similar to this.

The mechanism of UFOs is based on the relationship between this world and the spirit world. Therefore, once science on Earth is capable of becoming clear about the spirit world, we will be able to face extraterrestrials on an equal footing.

We are still a long way behind in our scientific technology, however, so if the extraterrestrials were to do whatever they liked, we would be helpless to do anything about it. It would be similar to the time when Europeans like Columbus first discovered the West Indies and later the American continent; the European civilization was so advanced that they were able to do as they liked.

That is why Professor Stephen Hawking said something along the lines of "I do not want to believe in extraterrestrial life, because if there were aliens, we would be like the natives in the face of the white man's invasion. There would be a huge difference in our civilizations, and it is frightening just to think about so I prefer not to believe in them."

Aliens certainly have the technology to have their way with us, but they have not done so. In this respect, they are also part of the occult; aliens show us glimpses of their existence, but never reveal everything. They do abduct people on Earth but erase their memories so people will not be able to remember what happened during that time. Of course, if the victims are hypnotized they are able to recall everything that happened, and the extraterrestrials have already taken that into account. In the same way that religious leaders teach the philosophy of the spirit world, so the aliens let us know time and again that there exists a secret world in space and that extraterrestrials come from it to visit Earth.

Nevertheless they do not simply reveal all their secrets and there is a reason for this. They do not reveal everything so that we can seek answers for ourselves and uncover the truth.

You may worry that such a difference in our scientific technology allows them to do whatever they like. But in the universe, there is an organization similar to the United Nations on Earth, which sets rules for aliens to abide by, preventing them from going beyond certain limits. Moreover, there are beings in Earth's spirit group who are involved in matters relating to the universe. Rient Arl Croud, whom I mentioned earlier, is in charge of intergalactic relations and Confucius is another nine-dimensional spirit who is currently involved in this issue.

When extraterrestrials come to Earth, they are given boundaries as to what they can and cannot do. They are not permitted to act as they please, so, ultimately, there is no real need for worry. We are not in danger of being completely annihilated by extraterrestrials.

Life forms in the third dimension, that is to say, creatures with physical bodies, are an extremely valuable resource for the universe. There are countless souls in the universe whose physical bodies have perished and who are unable to find suitable bodies to inhabit. When this happens, they need to move to another planet to find new bodies they can use. For this reason, physical bodies are an important resource in the universe and they must be preserved.

Sometimes the extraterrestrials come to Earth and negotiate to use our bodies, but there are limits to that as well. Promises are made and negotiations carried out in each case. At present, they are not allowed to intervene any more than the extent of our revelations of mysticism, so I would like you all to rest assured of this.

4
To Reveal What is Hidden

As can be seen from what I have written so far, there are several major challenges for us from the twenty-first century onward, including how to discover the relationship between the third dimension and higher dimensions, and to what extent we will be able to use that discovery as technology to travel between dimensions. Other issues include whether this information will be taught in schools as standardized knowledge and, when it is, whether even more hidden facts about the occult will be revealed.

It will take time to uncover all the secrets, as each mystery that is clarified will keep presenting new mysteries. I believe that *The Laws of the Sun* has unveiled much of the truth, but there are actually still a great number of unrevealed secrets. *The Laws of the Sun* only explains as much as is allowed and thought suitable for present-day humankind, and a great deal remains that is yet to be revealed.

As we spread Happy Science teachings, we cannot completely ignore the rules of this world, nor the rationality and commonly accepted knowledge of this world, otherwise we will be confronted with persecution and unable to continue our mission for long. Therefore a certain degree of compromise, of rationalization, and a willingness to conform to commonly accepted knowledge are necessary. In this context, Happy Science's teachings of the occult are still limited. If I were to reveal all the truths about the mysteries of this world, it would contradict the facts of this world in many ways. That is why I am limiting my teachings to a certain extent, to be able to harmonize with this world.

To be honest, I am currently using less than 10 percent of my inherent ability to avoid conflict with the world. Some people may be able to be tolerant with me when I say that I am able to converse with spirits or talk to people's guardian spirits. But how about if I say that I am able to understand the conversations of the crows or listen to the fish talking while they swim in a pond?

In fact, the world I live in is full of such mysteries. I can hear the conversations of birds and I am even able to understand the emotions and thoughts of animals and insects. If I take this too far, however, I will find that, although I can understand everything in the universe, my life here in this world will become exceedingly difficult. That is why I am managing Happy Science in a way that can be harmonious with human society to a certain degree.

Still, as the number of believers increases, the part of our teachings that has been hidden as occultism will gradually be revealed.

5
Humans Possess Spiritual Organs

All human beings possess spiritual organs to some degree. While the human body is a physical being, it actually has numerous spiritual organs. The brow between a person's eyebrows is one example of this. In the Lotus Sutra, it is written that Shakyamuni Buddha emitted a beam of white light from his brow. This white light is also depicted in our film, *The Laws of the Sun*. The brow is a spot where strong willpower, one of the spiritual functions that is extremely creative and positive, can be emitted.

The eyes are also spiritual organs. People speak of "the opening of the spiritual eyes" and, simply by looking at someone's eyes, it is possible to see if their spiritual eyes are open. When my spiritual eyes opened, I could see in a mirror that my eyes had changed. When the spiritual eyes are open, they seem to possess an extra gleam of light inside. When the eyes have attained this gleam, it becomes possible to see spiritual things—you will be able to discern people's auras and spirit bodies. You will be able to sense people's thought waves so, if someone thinks of you intensely, then you will come to see that person as clearly as if they were there with you.

Among those whose spiritual eyes have opened are some who can see me in a spiritual way. For instance, when I traveled to America or Europe, there were people in those countries who were able to see me spiritually.

The nose is another spiritual organ. While there are not so many people who put their nose to spiritual use, some are able to discern spiritual smells. They are able to discern a bad smell when an evil spirit appears or when a person possessed by an evil spirit approaches them, even though there is no actual smell. Spirits from Hell can sometimes be recognized by the terrible smell they have; it is a unique smell, like a mixture of slums and river mud. On the other hand, when angels appear, some people notice a beautiful fragrance in the air. Modern people generally have a poor sense of smell, but some people are able to discern these smells.

There was a time when Kung Fu actor Bruce Lee was said to have appeared as a ghost after he had died. It seems that, at that time, a terrible smell accompanied his spirit, so it was widely rumored that he had fallen to Hell.

The area from the throat to the mouth is used when giving lectures and this area also emits a large quantity of light. Light comes forth in the form of words, so this area, too, can be said to be a spiritual organ. My lectures are recorded each time and even when they are played back later, the image and the voice reproduce the spiritual power. Even if a lecture was given a year ago or even ten years ago, if somebody possessed by an evil spirit watches it, the evil spirit will suddenly become violent or leave that person, trying to escape the light. This is indeed an incredible phenomenon.

How is it possible to preserve spiritual power as a recording and replay it at a later date? In fact, the spiritual power emitted during my lectures is recorded as image and sound, thereby "translated" into something of this world, but when it is played back, the high-dimensional power that belongs to the worlds beyond the fourth dimension is reproduced. As for the actual mechanism of this process, I hope that researchers of electro-technology will study and clarify it.

The opposite can also happen. When I see somebody who is possessed by an evil spirit or an even stronger malicious spirit on television or in a video, these spirits sometimes visit me. The same also happens with photographs, and if the person in the photograph is already dead, I know immediately. This phenomenon occurs with screen images and photographs.

The palm of the hand also possesses a spiritual chakra from which light can be emitted. Healing power often flows from here, and by laying hands on someone, that person can be cured of illness. A positive power comes from the palm of the hand and some people can sense this power. Sometimes this power is used to heal wounds and the wounds can actually be healed. In olden times, people often used this power. As long as a person's mind is harmonious, the palm of their hand emits healing power.

The heart is another spiritual organ. The heart is easily influenced by outside emotions and is able to perceive other people's feelings directly. On the other hand, if people develop a strong will, they are able to influence those around them. So the heart possesses great spiritual power.

The *tanden*, which is located in the lower belly, is also a major spiritual center. Harmonizing the mind by maintaining a serene heart and patience is a very important practice in religions, and the spiritual center of this power to harmonize the mind is found in the *tanden*.

In the area below the stomach are the sex organs. The man has a male organ and testicles while women have female organs and a womb. These are also spiritual organs that emit spiritual power. Since ancient times, many religions have preached sexual taboos, and one of the reasons is the relationship between sexual desire and spiritual ability.

When people's vitality and sexual desire are low, they are unable to prevent evil spirits from attacking them. As their vitality declines, so does their power of resistance to evil spirits. On the other hand, when their sexual power is at its peak, they can emit a strong willpower; they are in a good condition to create a spiritual field to produce such power.

I presume that people in olden times were well aware of this fact. Today people eat high-calorie diets that allow them to restore their energy quickly. In the past, however, people's diets were much lower in calories and they could only build up a store of energy little by little. Therefore, unless they controlled their sexual energies wisely, they would be unable to emit power for spiritual use. That is why sexual abstinence was recommended.

If you practice sexual abstinence, you can build up spiritual power. In esoteric religions or yoga, this is referred to as *kundalini*, which literally means "coiled," and it refers to the energy the sexual chakra exerts. It really is a powerful force. If this energy is used for good purposes, it can be a great power to blast away evil spirits or help someone advance in enlightenment, but if used for wrong purposes, it can be a destructive power. So it has both a positive and a negative power.

In this way, human bodies have numerous spiritual organs and everyone is influenced in some way or other. If you make a conscious effort to develop these areas, they will produce much more power.

It is true that human beings are affected by material and physical things while they are in this world, but they are simultaneously open to spiritual influences. We are living under the influence of both these factors. In this respect, we are similar to the beings in an aquarium inside a room. Beings in an aquarium are affected not only by what happens inside the tank, but also by what happens in the room. Please understand your life in this way.

6
Mysticism Gives People Courage and Power to Overcome their Limits

In this chapter, I have spoken about occultism as a power in many ways and I would like to end by suggesting that you should not be too concerned about how the world sees you for being too involved in occultism. There are many mystical phenomena in this world, but, by believing in mysticism, you will be able to release your true power that has been bound by commonly accepted knowledge. The power that has been suppressed within you will come out. It is important to release this power. Moreover, by opening your eyes to the world that exists beyond this one, you will be able to discover a greater self and you will find that courage wells up from within.

You should not be surprised to learn that civilizations such as Atlantis and Mu have existed in the past. There have been other, even older great civilizations on Earth. When we think of these civilizations that existed in the far distant past, the various worries of the mundane world will seem fairly petty. You will come to realize how you have been making so much fuss about small, insignificant matters. If you limit your outlook to this world, there will be any number of things that will cause you worry, but if you go beyond it, then you will find yourself with greater strength.

In this respect, as a religion, Happy Science must be determined to believe in occultism as a power. The occult and mysticism have the power to provide people with courage, to encourage them to break through their limits, and to bring about miracles while creating supernatural phenomena. This is not something ridiculous but the true nature of the universe. Believing in the occult is equal to developing and exerting true human power, which is confined to one-tenth of its real potential. If religion has come to an impasse in this world, it is necessary to return to its starting point.

Chapter Five

What it Means to Believe

~ Go Beyond the Boundaries between This World and the Next ~

Lecture given on October 6, 2001

1

The Three Ways of Life of The Guiding Spirits of Light

I would like to conclude this book by discussing the theme "What It Means to Believe." Religions grow and develop over time in a variety of ways, but sometimes it is necessary to return to the origin, or the essence, of religions, the part that can be explained in the simplest words. To answer the various needs of this world, the teachings of a religion may become diverse and complex, but what is closest to the origin will last the longest, and the universal and somewhat abstract teachings will remain in the end.

Let us start by thinking about the lives of the Guiding Spirits of Light. Guiding Spirits of Light come down from the heavenly world to be born on Earth, where they accomplish various work before returning to the other world. The way they lead their lives on Earth can be divided roughly into three types.

First, there are Guiding Spirits of Light who are not accepted in this world and lead difficult lives, filled with disappointment. Their efforts are only recognized in later years, or perhaps after they die, and their teachings gradually come to be valued over a long time. These people are usually so far ahead of their time that they are not understood by their contemporaries. Moreover, because these people are extremely spiritual, the gap between their teachings and the secular world is too wide for the average person to accept or understand them.

The second type is those who exert their powers as Guiding Spirits of Light and carry out, to a certain extent, different sorts of work that result in some social recognition. At a certain point in time, however, they encounter conflicts with this world and end up failing, unable to accomplish fully their original mission. In the midst of adversity or in disappointment, they painfully give their teachings, like silkworms producing silk, placing their hope in their teachings and leaving them for disciples to spread in the future. In that they eventually come to be understood by others, they are similar to the first type of Guiding Spirits.

The third type consists of those who are successful in a worldly sense; they gain recognition while they are still alive. Their way of life is respected both by their contemporaries and by future generations.

Guiding Spirits of Light lead one of these three types of lives while on Earth. I would now like to analyze these three ways of life in more detail.

The first way of life is extremely spiritual. It seems almost strange that these teachers dwell in a human body, live in the material world, and have to eat. I think that it is quite common for religious people to live in ways that are not accepted by others from the very beginning. There is quite a large number of this type and many of the prophets of the Old Testament belong to this group. Jesus Christ could also be considered to belong to this category. If we look at the two thousand years of history that followed Christ, we see that there have been many religious leaders whose way of life was not accepted at all while they were alive but who were recognized later on. This type of person inevitably exists in religion.

The second type is accepted to a certain degree, but others are unable to follow them to the very end. This type's path is obstructed by worldly barriers, and their lives end in misfortune. Confucius is an example of this type. He achieved a certain degree of worldly success but experienced setbacks and, in the end, left his teachings only to his close disciples. So this type of person will achieve a certain degree of worldly success, perhaps even become a government minister, but will ultimately be unable to deliver their entire teaching. They are not understood by people and, in the end, only those who can understand their teachings will pass on their message.

The third type is people who are active as leaders in this world. They enter politics, business, or the academic world, succeed in their respective fields, and achieve their potential. There are a fair amount of people of this type.

It is difficult to say which of these ways of living is more spiritual or religious than the other, but, roughly speaking, these are the three types. What is more, if we break them down further, the first type can be split into two subtypes. One is the type who meets with strong rejection and leads a tragic life without ever being accepted.

People in the other subtype cut themselves off from society voluntarily, becoming "dropouts" and living in a leisurely way in their own world. Many Buddhist priests belong to this category. They move into the mountains and isolate themselves from society, just like the Japanese monk Ryokan. Many ascetics of old belonged to this group as well. These people do not influence this world in any way, preferring to live in their own world. This way of life is also to be found in the philosophies of Lao-tzu and Chuang-tzu, founders of Taoism.

There is nothing tragic about this lifestyle. Although such people have disengaged from this world, they simply create their own spiritual world here on Earth. If these people were to be classified as a separate type, it could be said there are four ways of life for Guiding Spirits of Light here on Earth.

2

A Reversal of Values

Two contradictory sets of values

Guiding Spirits of Light have high levels of awareness, but why do we find these Guiding Spirits of Light among those who distance themselves from this world or live lives full of tragedy and misery? There is only one fundamental reason: their set of values is a complete reversal of earthly values.

Before they are born, all people know their true nature and the true way of life. Once people are born and grow up on Earth, however, they gradually forget these things. By the time a person reaches the age of about ten, the ego starts to form. They recognize themselves as an independent individual and start working to create a better and more comfortable life for themselves in this world.

In a worldly sense, this is a process of growth and a way to perfection as a human, but it is simultaneously a process of forgetting your existence as a spiritual being. If you feel that this world is more comfortable and more enjoyable to live in, and if you find that your life goes exactly as you want, you will become more and more engrossed in it.

As you grow older, however, your body becomes infirm and you are no longer able to move as freely as when you were young. Your body feels heavy, as if you were wearing armor, and everything becomes an effort. Your back becomes round, wrinkles appear, your hair turns gray and eventually falls out. You cannot speak as expressively as you once did, your memory fades, and you become forgetful. Life becomes very difficult for you.

Aging is a painful process in a worldly sense, but, as a result, this world will no longer appear a comfortable place to live. This process is akin to returning to your infancy. It is said that as you grow older, you regress and become like an infant again. The fact that the world becomes harder to live in means you are returning to your original starting point. As you return to your original starting point, you will realize that the time is nearing for you to bid farewell to this world.

In this world, it is considered good to work to establish your ego and develop your individuality as you grow up. I agree with this, as it is part of your spiritual discipline in this world. However, you must know that, at the same time, it means you are forgetting and growing further away from your original being.

After a certain age, your body weakens and you become unable to move freely or do as you want, but you begin simultaneously to feel that perhaps this world is no longer the place for you. You will then feel like there is another place waiting for you and gradually you will be attracted to that world.

So there are two contradictory values in this world. In order to be successful and become a competent person in this world, it is necessary to perfect yourself as an individual human being. The more you strive in this direction, however, the more cut off you will be from the other world and the more you will forget your spiritual self.

The philosophy of egolessness
Taught by Shakyamuni Buddha

Keeping in mind what I have said so far, I would now like to consider the philosophy of egolessness taught by Shakyamuni Buddha. As we reach the age of ten, we naturally start developing our ego and this is true of everybody. People will fight, attack, and sometimes kill others to protect themselves. They may also fight over food. Since it is important to survive, it is natural to enter the world of ego and people do so without ever being taught.

In worldly terms, the development of the ego is considered to be part of the process of growing up. The philosophy of egolessness completely contradicts this, however.

At first glance, it appears as if people who adhere to a philosophy of egolessness lose out in this world of strife. In a world of warring egos, somebody who believes in a philosophy of egolessness will appear to be a good sacrifice or prey. They will appear to be easy game; anyone would think they did not stand a chance of winning.

A person who has fully achieved the egoless state of mind, however, has the power to make others reflect on their thoughts and actions, causing them to repent. An egoless person will make others feel the emptiness of hurting each other to protect their own egos, of fighting and holding others back as they pursue their own success. They will come to realize that learning the philosophy of egolessness, even a part of it, will make their lives easier.

This philosophy of egolessness has a similar effect as the teachings of Zen Buddhism, a sect that emerged from the stream of Buddhism. Practitioners use a strong reprimand or words of wisdom to awaken people and instantly change their way of thinking. The philosophy of egolessness has a similar power.

Having said this, however, while living in this world, it is impossible to let go of your own ego completely and become fully egoless. In the same way that it is impossible to get rid of basic human desires completely while living in a physical body, the ego cannot be completely erased. In fact, many people are unable to get rid of their egos even after dying, after shedding their physical body and becoming spirit. It is extremely difficult to extinguish the ego.

If somebody dared to teach the philosophy of egolessness and taught a reversal of values, however, people would come to feel a need to study these teachings and work to control their egos even slightly. Then more people would follow suit. Thus the first buds of harmony, of Utopia, would appear.

To put it another way, if people live in this world solely from their instincts, they will only advance in the direction of amplifying their egos, but when they come into contact with somebody who preaches a complete reversal of values, they will be able to awaken to a completely different thinking. In a certain context, the discovery of this philosophy will lead them closer to the other world again. This is the philosophy of egolessness.

Achieve a higher degree of self-realization By abandoning the self

Egolessness can be described in other words as the "abandonment of self." "Abandonment of self" means to cast off your lowly self, the self that is attached to this material world and suffers agonies, to attain a higher self. By abandoning the desire to take from others, you will be able to achieve a higher degree of self-realization. Those who abandon the most will gain the most.

What kind of people are considered to have abandoned the most? They are the ones who devoted their limited life to other people, whether for decades or one hundred years. By doing this, the life they used for others will accomplish far greater work through the lives of other people; thus their life will resurrect in this world on a greater scale.

Those who use their limited life solely for their own sake will never achieve anything beyond that life. However, those who use the decades of their limited life for the sake of others, those who devote 50, 60, 70, 80, 90, 99, or even 100 percent of their life to other people, will find that their life produces tens or hundreds of times more than what can be achieved in one lifetime.

So then, what kind of people are able to achieve this? At the very least, those who base their lives on worldly values will not be able to devote themselves to altruistic goals. Many of the people who appear to be altruistic, although their values are rooted in this world, are hypocrites. They generally do good things solely out of vanity or desire for fame, to win praise, or to make themselves look good.

People who are truly able to abandon themselves are spiritual people and they are loved by Buddha or God. They have a pure heart that is attuned to Buddha or God. Otherwise, they would not be able to live that kind of life.

In general, people who live according to their instincts work to expand themselves or their egos, believing that this is the principle of success. From a worldly perspective, it certainly seems as if they would otherwise lose to others and feel a failure. However, if they wish to achieve greater victory, a real victory, they have to do a complete turnaround in outlook.

Those who live for as many people as possible, who are willing to abandon their life for others, will achieve a rich harvest. They will be able to gain ten, a hundred, even a thousand times more life, making the best use of the life that has been given to them by God or Buddha.

3
From Worldly Success to Religious Enlightenment

As I stated earlier, even Guiding Spirits of Light have three or four different ways of living in this world, but we cannot say which way of life will allow them to fulfill their mission and bring true happiness. It all depends on the aptitudes of an individual.

People who are able to guide others while achieving success in this world have a comparatively high level of rationality, intelligence, and physical endurance. They need to be careful not to allow themselves to become overly immersed in worldly success and forget their true self. Remember that many of the seeds of failure can be found in success.

Others are people who succeed in achieving a certain degree of worldly success but experience a setback and seek self-realization through a religious path. Quite a large percentage of these people can be found in religious organizations. When these people lead a religious life, they must be careful not to use their religious activities as a way of diverting their complaints or discontent with this world, or their greed at not knowing contentment. They must not forever complain and criticize others in the religion out of dissatisfaction at being unable to achieve success in this world.

Even if you have experienced unhappiness in your life, it is important that you always strive to purify your heart so that your mind is not clouded by your experiences. You may only have managed to achieve a 50 or 80 percent success, but even if you have only half succeeded, you should not merely bewail your situation. Rather, praise yourself on having got so far without losing your spiritual outlook on the world. This is something to be thankful for. So it is time for you to return to your original self and devote yourself to spiritual discipline. You must know that being away from the secular world, attacking and criticizing the world out of personal resentment, will not lead you to any spiritual progress.

The last category is the people who live in completely unworldly ways, whose lives appear tragic and wretched, or who cut themselves off from society. This kind of life is very difficult and these people will rarely be understood by others. It requires a certain bent to live in this way and not everybody is capable of it.

People who try to live this kind of life will face difficulties in this world before fulfilling their mission; they will be criticized, pressured, persecuted, slandered, and endure prejudice. Perhaps they will lose their financial foothold, their health may be impaired, and they may be confronted by all kinds of problems. There are very few people who have enough conviction to overcome such difficulties and continue advancing while rejecting worldly values.

Therefore, for the majority of people, the best way is to pursue success as ordinary people and transform their experiences into religious awakening and higher enlightenment in the course of their lives.

4

The Science of the Spirit World

The meaning of "science"
In the name "Happy Science"

I would like you all to understand the meaning of "science" in the name "Happy Science." In this context, "science" does not refer to the natural sciences or empirical studies; rather, it refers to the science of faith or the science of believing. This is a science that studies the laws of the mind. It is a study of the workings of the mind. It is a science exploring the Laws that run through this world to the next.

Therefore it is not a science that believes only in matter that can be physically seen, heard, or touched. It is not a science that believes only in facts that are proved by conducting the same experiment tens or even hundreds of times. Our science is based on a world that cannot be seen, heard, or touched. Hardly anyone has ever traveled to that unseen world and come back. Despite this, I continue to teach that the other world is the true world, and that the world in which we now live is only a temporary abode, a tiny world that exists within a much vaster space.

Judged by what people learn and experience in this world, what I am saying may sound absurd because most people have never before studied the other world. Rather than believing in my teachings, it is much easier to believe that advanced human civilization has existed for only the last few thousand years. Life would be much easier to live if you could blindly believe that, long ago, random proteins clumped together and developed into organisms such as lizards, frogs, birds, butterflies, insects, or even mammals like whales or humans.

When seen from a much greater perspective of the world, however, such theories are impossible to believe. Nevertheless there are many happily ignorant people today who believe in these theories. People today have undergone a kind of brainwashing by modern science, which has become their religion. In other words, people are taught to believe only in what can be proved through scientific formulas of chemistry or physics, and that anything that has not been proved does not exist.

The truth is, however, that what is now believed as "fact" is not really proven fact; it is almost impossible to research anything fully. Scientists are only making assumptions based on calculations or evidence. They can use calculations to indicate that, for example, the Big Bang happened at a certain time, but no matter how hard physics twists and turns, it cannot figure out how matter was created out of void. The answers to such subjects exist beyond this world and can only be found in the realm of faith, the world of Buddha or God.

The same can be said of human beings. Animals may indeed evolve to suit their environment in this world, but a building is not constructed by chance, even if the materials are scattered all over the floor. In this world, such a thing is impossible. Anybody who has ever built a house understands this. If you place cement, water, gravel, bricks, and steel girders in an open space and leave them there for one hundred or one thousand years, will the house build itself? No, it will not. In order to build a house, somebody must first wish to build a house, draw up a blueprint, and bring together the efforts of people involved in the actual construction. Without these, a house can never be built.

The same is true of humans. Humans were created only because there was a being that desired to create humanity and made the effort to achieve this wish. There is no other possibility except this.

Therefore, in the name of science, there is a science that tries to deny faith, as well as a much grander science, the science of the spirit world, which attempts to go beyond worldly matters. I would like all of you to be aware of this.

Modern humankind has lost its original powers

In order to teach people about the science of the spirit world, we must create a movement to bring about a reversal of values. To make this happen, we need people whose actions may seem mad in light of the values of this world, people who might look eccentric or odd and become the butt of laughter in this world. These people appear strange, however, only because the people of this world have become immersed in a mistaken way of thinking.

When you were at school and studied classical literature, you may have come across stories about ghosts or spirits of the living. Modern people tend to scorn such things, considering them to belong to a primitive age, but once your spiritual eyes have opened, you will know that they really do exist and are exactly as described. In this sense, it is difficult to say which is the more advanced, ancient times when these stories were written or the present day.

At the very least, people of the past were able to feel or experience in their daily lives the workings of other people's minds, their willpower, and the spirit world. Today, however, people are incapable of sensing such things; their senses have become extremely dull.

People today may have developed new abilities, but, at the same time, they have lost many of the abilities humans used to possess. What has been lost is not the abilities of primitive peoples; these are the abilities that are regained after they die and leave their bodies behind, these are their original abilities.

Contemporary people have lost their original powers, and they try to establish themselves only within the rules of this world. This is a sad situation because it means the majority of people are living a mistaken way of life. If we were to decide now by majority vote what truth is, real spiritual truth would not be chosen.

That would be fine, however. If spiritual truths were supported by the majority, they would be considered to be rational ideas, and if these rational ideas were proven, everybody would accept them easily and there would be no room for the arising of faith. Faith becomes essential because the majority in this world do not support spiritual truth.

5

Go Beyond the Boundaries between This World and the Other

Why we need the power of faith

Faith is the power to go beyond the boundaries between this world and the other world. It is our weapon for going beyond the wall that stands between these two worlds.

Through belief, it is possible to break through the wall between the dimensions. With the power of faith, we can transcend the dimensional boundaries and, as a result, many things will come and go between these dimensions. We can bring back different kinds of power, and this world and the other will become one.

When you live with a strong faith, you are living in the multidimensional world while you are still alive in the third dimension. When you have a strong faith, you are living in the heavenly world, for instance in the Realm of Tathagatas, the Realm of Bodhisattvas, the Realm of Light, and the Realm of Good.

Likewise, people whose minds are filled with strong evil thoughts will find that their minds are connected to Hell while they are still living on Earth. In the world of the mind, these people are linked with Hell and have created an open passageway between the two worlds. There are numerous misguided faiths in the world today that create this sort of access between this world and Hell.

Therefore it is vital to understand the following. It is important that the righteous succeed and that righteousness be recognized in this world. I hope this will come true. It is not always possible for this to manifest, however. In this world, sometimes the righteous can be defeated by what is mistaken or evil, but this is just how the world operates. This world has been created as a kind of an experiment ground where it is difficult to understand what is right. It is a place where our souls are tested. For this reason, you must never forget that the veracity of a religion is never based solely on its success or failure in this world.

You need the power of faith because the fundamental principles of this world are different from those of the other world. That is why you need the strength to overcome such differences. At such times, faith becomes indispensable.

Endurance supports faith

You may ask how to support or uphold faith, and the answer is through the power to endure. People's thoughts will come true; they will come true without fail. It takes a certain amount of time for thoughts to be realized, however, and the means and methods by which this is achieved are not always what you expect at the beginning. This is something that you have to accept.

In this world, your thoughts may not manifest in the most ideal way, and sometimes they will manifest in the way that is second or third best for you. People whom you thought would help you may turn you down, while you may receive support from somebody you least expected to give it. People you had regarded as enemies may turn out to be supporters, while your friends may become your enemies.

In this world, you cannot entirely have your way with money, land, buildings, or other matters, and your thoughts may be realized in a different form than you expected. Nonetheless, wishes that you hold strongly in your heart will gradually be realized. There are many different ways and means by which they will come true, but they will manifest in the end.

In times of struggle, as a person with faith, it is vital to have the power to endure. You must be able to endure. It is through endurance that your thoughts will be realized.

Please be aware that, in the end, the results of faith do not always have to manifest in your lifetime. If your belief does not manifest in this world, it can also mean that you have a deep, strong, and sublime faith.

When you do not succeed right away, it is easy to stop believing, but you must remember that there are people who dream of success several hundred years or even several thousand years into the future. Time alone will tell if such hopes are crazy or sane.

Have stronger faith and courage

Nearly twenty years [at the time of the lecture] have passed since Happy Science first began its activities. I feel that we have won greater recognition and success than we expected, and received the support of more people than we first anticipated. This is something for which I am most grateful.

I sometimes worry, however, that my teachings are being accepted by such large numbers of people in this world because not much faith is required when joining Happy Science. This unease sometimes crosses my heart. In one sense, the way I give my teachings and the way we spread them may still be too worldly. But in order to guide all people in the world, a much stronger faith is required.

The ability to cooperate and harmonize with others is quite a beneficial weapon in this world, but if this ability limits and weakens our activities, we will never grow any bigger. We must ask ourselves if we have become complacent with the small group of people who understand and value our movement. The vast majority of people still do not believe in Happy Science, but if we forget about these people and are satisfied with the narrow range of people who share our views, then the masses will simply look upon us as a harmless group and ignore us. That is not what I came here to accomplish, however.

A religion that receives general acceptance sometimes loses the power to develop any further. We must always introduce new themes, provide the people of the world with new stimuli, and urge a reversal of values. Unless we repeatedly give out this energy, we will not be able to become a powerful force in the truest sense, or prosper into the twenty-first century and beyond.

I have spoken about a variety of subjects, but if I were to sum up this chapter in one phrase, it would be: "Believing is going beyond the dimensional boundaries between this world and the other." There are clearly dimensional boundaries between this world and the other world, and ordinary people are incapable of transcending them.

What enables us to go beyond them is the act of faith. To truly understand and master faith, you must go beyond these boundaries.

Going beyond these boundaries is accompanied by

pain. It requires endurance. Once you have overcome these things, however, you will, for the first time, become someone who is not of this world while still alive in it.

In Buddhism, a person whose mind is attuned to the other world is known as an *arhat*, and in Christianity, a saint. You will be able to enter the world in which they live. It is my dearest wish that all of you will gain more courage and achieve this.

Afterword

It takes courage to produce a best seller that contains the sort of material found in this book. Any businessperson will tell you this.

To build trust for my words, I have published almost four hundred books.* On the basis of trust, I have tackled the difficult challenge of revealing the mystical truths of the great universe.

I believe that once you have finished reading this book, you will find it impossible to return to your old self, for you have now learned the secrets that run through this world and the other.

When you have learned of what has been hidden, will you feel guilt or will you find courage welling up from within? Whichever you experience, you can be sure that the train of life you are riding will take a completely new track.

Ryuho Okawa
Founder and CEO of Happy Science Group
Autumn 2004

---

* As of the end of December 2014, the number of books published reached 1,800.

ABOUT THE AUTHOR

Founder and CEO of Happy Science Group.

Ryuho Okawa was born on July 7th 1956, in Tokushima, Japan. After graduating from the University of Tokyo with a law degree, he joined a Tokyo-based trading house. While working at its New York headquarters, he studied international finance at the Graduate Center of the City University of New York. In 1981, he attained Great Enlightenment and became aware that he is El Cantare with a mission to bring salvation to all humankind.

In 1986, he established Happy Science. It now has members in over 165 countries across the world, with more than 700 branches and temples as well as 10,000 missionary houses around the world.

He has given over 3,450 lectures (of which more than 150 are in English) and published over 3,000 books (of which more than 600 are Spiritual Interview Series), and many are translated into 40 languages. Along with *The Laws of the Sun* and *The Laws Of Messiah*, many of the books have become best sellers or million sellers. To date, Happy Science has produced 25 movies. The original story and original concept were given by the Executive Producer Ryuho Okawa. He has also composed music and written lyrics of over 450 pieces.

Moreover, he is the Founder of Happy Science University and Happy Science Academy (Junior and Senior High School), Founder and President of the Happiness Realization Party, Founder and Honorary Headmaster of Happy Science Institute of Government and Management, Founder of IRH Press Co., Ltd., and the Chairperson of NEW STAR PRODUCTION Co., Ltd. and ARI Production Co., Ltd.

WHAT IS EL CANTARE?

El Cantare means "the Light of the Earth," and is the Supreme God of the Earth who has been guiding humankind since the beginning of Genesis. He is whom Jesus called Father and Muhammad called Allah, and is *Ame-no-Mioya-Gami*, Japanese Father God. Different parts of El Cantare's core consciousness have descended to Earth in the past, once as Alpha and another as Elohim. His branch spirits, such as Shakyamuni Buddha and Hermes, have descended to Earth many times and helped to flourish many civilizations. To unite various religions and to integrate various fields of study in order to build a new civilization on Earth, a part of the core consciousness has descended to Earth as Master Ryuho Okawa.

Alpha is a part of the core consciousness of El Cantare who descended to Earth around 330 million years ago. Alpha preached Earth's Truths to harmonize and unify Earth-born humans and space people who came from other planets.

Elohim is a part of El Cantare's core consciousness who descended to Earth around 150 million years ago. He gave wisdom, mainly on the differences of light and darkness, good and evil.

Ame-no-Mioya-Gami (Japanese Father God) is the Creator God and the Father God who appears in the ancient literature, *Hotsuma Tsutae*. It is believed that He descended on the foothills of Mt. Fuji about 30,000 years ago and built the Fuji dynasty, which is the root of the Japanese civilization. With justice as the central pillar, Ame-no-Mioya-Gami's teachings spread to ancient civilizations of other countries in the world.

Shakyamuni Buddha was born as a prince into the Shakya Clan in India around 2,600 years ago. When he was 29 years old, he renounced the world and sought enlightenment. He later attained Great Enlightenment and founded Buddhism.

Hermes is one of the 12 Olympian gods in Greek mythology, but the spiritual Truth is that he taught the teachings of love and progress around 4,300 years ago that became the origin of the current Western civilization. He is a hero that truly existed.

Ophealis was born in Greece around 6,500 years ago and was the leader who took an expedition to as far as Egypt. He is the God of miracles, prosperity, and arts, and is known as Osiris in the Egyptian mythology.

Rient Arl Croud was born as a king of the ancient Incan Empire around 7,000 years ago and taught about the mysteries of the mind. In the heavenly world, he is responsible for the interactions that take place between various planets.

Thoth was an almighty leader who built the golden age of the Atlantic civilization around 12,000 years ago. In the Egyptian mythology, he is known as god Thoth.

Ra Mu was a leader who built the golden age of the civilization of Mu around 17,000 years ago. As a religious leader and a politician, he ruled by uniting religion and politics.

ABOUT HAPPY SCIENCE

Happy Science is a global movement that empowers individuals to find purpose and spiritual happiness and to share that happiness with their families, societies, and the world. With more than 12 million members around the world, Happy Science aims to increase awareness of spiritual truths and expand our capacity for love, compassion, and joy so that together we can create the kind of world we all wish to live in.

Activities at Happy Science are based on the Principle of Happiness (Love, Wisdom, Self-Reflection, and Progress). This principle embraces worldwide philosophies and beliefs, transcending boundaries of culture and religions.

Love teaches us to give ourselves freely without expecting anything in return; it encompasses giving, nurturing, and forgiving.

Wisdom leads us to the insights of spiritual truths, and opens us to the true meaning of life and the will of God (the universe, the highest power, Buddha).

Self-Reflection brings a mindful, nonjudgmental lens to our thoughts and actions to help us find our truest selves—the essence of our souls—and deepen our connection to the highest power. It helps us attain a clean and peaceful mind and leads us to the right life path.

Progress emphasizes the positive, dynamic aspects of our spiritual growth—actions we can take to manifest and spread happiness around the world. It's a path that not only expands our soul growth, but also furthers the collective potential of the world we live in.

PROGRAMS AND EVENTS

The doors of Happy Science are open to all. We offer a variety of programs and events, including self-exploration and self-growth programs, spiritual seminars, meditation and contemplation sessions, study groups, and book events.

Our programs are designed to:
* Deepen your understanding of your purpose and meaning in life
* Improve your relationships and increase your capacity to love unconditionally
* Attain peace of mind, decrease anxiety and stress, and feel positive
* Gain deeper insights and a broader perspective on the world
* Learn how to overcome life's challenges
  ... and much more.

For more information, visit <u>happy-science.org</u>.

CONTACT INFORMATION

Happy Science is a worldwide organization with branches and temples around the globe. For a comprehensive list, visit the worldwide directory at *happy-science.org*. The following are some of the many Happy Science locations:

UNITED STATES AND CANADA

New York
79 Franklin St., New York, NY 10013, USA
Phone: 1-212-343-7972
Fax: 1-212-343-7973
Email: ny@happy-science.org
Website: happyscience-usa.org

New Jersey
66 Hudson St., #2R, Hoboken, NJ 07030, USA
Phone: 1-201-313-0127
Email: nj@happy-science.org
Website: happyscience-usa.org

Chicago
2300 Barrington Rd., Suite #400,
Hoffman Estates, IL 60169, USA
Phone: 1-630-937-3077
Email: chicago@happy-science.org
Website: happyscience-usa.org

Florida
5208 8th St., Zephyrhills, FL 33542, USA
Phone: 1-813-715-0000
Fax: 1-813-715-0010
Email: florida@happy-science.org
Website: happyscience-usa.org

Atlanta
1874 Piedmont Ave., NE Suite 360-C
Atlanta, GA 30324, USA
Phone: 1-404-892-7770
Email: atlanta@happy-science.org
Website: happyscience-usa.org

San Francisco
525 Clinton St.
Redwood City, CA 94062, USA
Phone & Fax: 1-650-363-2777
Email: sf@happy-science.org
Website: happyscience-usa.org

Los Angeles
1590 E. Del Mar Blvd., Pasadena, CA
91106, USA
Phone: 1-626-395-7775
Fax: 1-626-395-7776
Email: la@happy-science.org
Website: happyscience-usa.org

Orange County
16541 Gothard St. Suite 104
Huntington Beach, CA 92647
Phone: 1-714-659-1501
Email: oc@happy-science.org
Website: happyscience-usa.org

San Diego
7841 Balboa Ave. Suite #202
San Diego, CA 92111, USA
Phone: 1-626-395-7775
Fax: 1-626-395-7776
E-mail: sandiego@happy-science.org
Website: happyscience-usa.org

Hawaii
Phone: 1-808-591-9772
Fax: 1-808-591-9776
Email: hi@happy-science.org
Website: happyscience-usa.org

Kauai
3343 Kanakolu Street, Suite 5
Lihue, HI 96766, USA
Phone: 1-808-822-7007
Fax: 1-808-822-6007
Email: kauai-hi@happy-science.org
Website: happyscience-usa.org

Toronto
845 The Queensway
Etobicoke, ON M8Z 1N6, Canada
Phone: 1-416-901-3747
Email: toronto@happy-science.org
Website: happy-science.ca

Vancouver
#201-2607 East 49th Avenue,
Vancouver, BC, V5S 1J9, Canada
Phone: 1-604-437-7735
Fax: 1-604-437-7764
Email: vancouver@happy-science.org
Website: happy-science.ca

INTERNATIONAL

Tokyo
1-6-7 Togoshi, Shinagawa,
Tokyo, 142-0041, Japan
Phone: 81-3-6384-5770
Fax: 81-3-6384-5776
Email: tokyo@happy-science.org
Website: happy-science.org

Seoul
74, Sadang-ro 27-gil,
Dongjak-gu, Seoul, Korea
Phone: 82-2-3478-8777
Fax: 82-2-3478-9777
Email: korea@happy-science.org
Website: happyscience-korea.org

London
3 Margaret St.
London, W1W 8RE United Kingdom
Phone: 44-20-7323-9255
Fax: 44-20-7323-9344
Email: eu@happy-science.org
Website: www.happyscience-uk.org

Taipei
No. 89, Lane 155, Dunhua N. Road,
Songshan District, Taipei City 105, Taiwan
Phone: 886-2-2719-9377
Fax: 886-2-2719-5570
Email: taiwan@happy-science.org
Website: happyscience-tw.org

Sydney
516 Pacific Highway, Lane Cove North,
2066 NSW, Australia
Phone: 61-2-9411-2877
Fax: 61-2-9411-2822
Email: sydney@happy-science.org

Kuala Lumpur
No 22A, Block 2, Jalil Link Jalan Jalil
Jaya 2, Bukit Jalil 57000,
Kuala Lumpur, Malaysia
Phone: 60-3-8998-7877
Fax: 60-3-8998-7977
Email: malaysia@happy-science.org
Website: happyscience.org.my

Sao Paulo
Rua. Domingos de Morais 1154,
Vila Mariana, Sao Paulo SP
CEP 04010-100, Brazil
Phone: 55-11-5088-3800
Email: sp@happy-science.org
Website: happyscience.com.br

Kathmandu
Kathmandu Metropolitan City,
Ward No. 15, Ring Road, Kimdol,
Sitapaila Kathmandu, Nepal
Phone: 977-1-427-2931
Email: nepal@happy-science.org

Jundiai
Rua Congo, 447, Jd. Bonfiglioli
Jundiai-CEP, 13207-340, Brazil
Phone: 55-11-4587-5952
Email: jundiai@happy-science.org

Kampala
Plot 877 Rubaga Road, Kampala
P.O. Box 34130 Kampala, UGANDA
Phone: 256-79-4682-121
Email: uganda@happy-science.org

ABOUT HS PRESS

HS Press is an imprint of IRH Press Co., Ltd. IRH Press Co., Ltd., based in Tokyo, was founded in 1987 as a publishing division of Happy Science. IRH Press publishes religious and spiritual books, journals, magazines and also operates broadcast and film production enterprises. For more information, visit *okawabooks.com*.

Follow us on:

f Facebook: Okawa Books   ⬛ Instagram: OkawaBooks
▶ Youtube: Okawa Books   🐦 Twitter: Okawa Books
P Pinterest: Okawa Books   g Goodreads: Ryuho Okawa

——— **NEWSLETTER** ———

To receive book related news, promotions and events, please subscribe to our newsletter below.

🔗 eepurl.com/bsMeJj

——— **AUDIO / VISUAL MEDIA** ———

YOUTUBE

PODCAST

Introduction of Ryuho Okawa's titles; topics ranging from self-help, current affairs, spirituality, religion, and the universe.

BOOKS BY RYUHO OKAWA

THE LAWS OF WISDOM
SHINE YOUR DIAMOND WITHIN

This book guides you along the path on how to acquire wisdom, so that you can break through any wall you are or will confront in your life or in your business. By reading this book, you will be able to avoid getting lost in the flood of information and, going beyond the level of just amassing knowledge, be able to come up with many great ideas, make effective planning and strategy and develop your leadership while receiving good inspiration.

THE LAWS OF PERSEVERANCE
REVERSING YOUR COMMON SENSE

"No matter how much you suffer, the Truth will gradually shine forth as you continue to endure hardships. Therefore, simply strengthen your mind and keep making constant efforts in times of endurance, however ordinary they may be."

-From Postscript

THE LAWS OF GREAT ENLIGHTENMENT
ALWAYS WALK WITH BUDDHA

In this modern society, people often find themselves unable to forgive someone and maintain a peaceful mind. However, there are ways to lead a stress-free life and enjoy happiness from within. This book offers the practical approaches to achieve it. By understanding the Buddhist concept "enlightenment", you will gain the power to forgive sins and get to know how to be the master of your own mind, not a slave to your emotions.

For a complete list of books, visit okawabooks.com

THE LAWS OF THE SUN

ONE SOURCE, ONE PLANET, ONE PEOPLE

IMAGINE IF YOU COULD ASK GOD why He created this world and what spiritual laws He used to shape us—and everything around us. If we could understand His designs and intentions, we could discover what our goals in life should be and whether our actions move us closer to those goals or farther away.

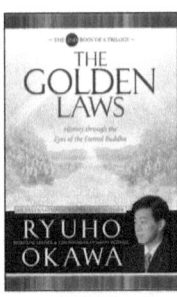

THE GOLDEN LAWS

HISTORY THROUGH THE EYES OF THE ETERNAL BUDDHA

The Golden Laws reveals how Buddha's Plan has been unfolding on earth, and outlines five thousand years of the secret history of humankind. Once we understand the true course of history, we cannot help but become aware of the significance of our spiritual mission in the present age.

THE NINE DIMENSIONS

UNVEILING THE LAWS OF ETERNITY

This book is a window into the mind of our loving God, who encourages us to grow into greater angels. It reveals His deepest intentions, answering the timely question of why He conceived such a colorful medley of religions, philosophies, sciences, arts, and other forms of expression.

For a complete list of books, visit okawabooks.com

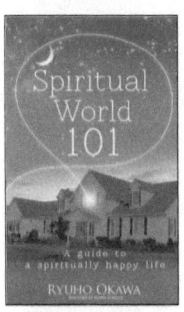

SPIRITUAL WORLD 101

A GUIDE TO A SPIRITUALLY HAPPY LIFE

This book is a spiritual guidebook that will answer all your questions about the spiritual world, with illustrations and diagrams explaining about your guardian spirit and the secrets of God and Buddha. By reading this book, you will be able to understand the true meaning of life and find happiness in everyday life.

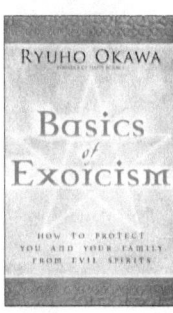

BASICS OF EXORCISM

HOW TO PROTECT YOU AND YOUR FAMILY FROM EVIL SPIRITS

No matter how much time progresses, demons are real. Unhappiness and misfortune in life caused by possession. Spiritual background behind schizophrenia and multiple personality.
Spiritual screen against curses – the truth of exorcism as told by the author who possesses the six great supernatural powers – The essence of exorcism as a result of more than 5000 rounds of exorcist experience!

MIRACULOUS WAYS TO CONQUER CANCER

AWAKEN TO THE POWER OF HEALING WITHIN YOU

Why do people get cancer? Why does the number of patients with cancer keep increasing in spite of medical progress? This book reveals how the mind creates cancer and the keys to overcome illnesses. Drive out cancer from your life!

For a complete list of books, visit okawabooks.com

Spiritual Messages from the Guardian Spirit of Ryuho Okawa

The Divine Voice of Shakyamuni Buddha

"The final goal is to realize what you call a 'Buddhaland Utopia.' Of course, this is not an easy task. However, it is important that you keep on making efforts to get close to it, generation after generation."

— Shakyamuni Buddha, Okawa's Guardian spirit

In Love with the Sun

Spiritual Messages from Goddess Gaia

After 600 million years, people shall know the true genesis. The true story when the earth was born, the guiding concept of the earth, the mechanism of creating life on Earth. And the future that human beings has to seek, these secrets are now revealed by the spiritual message from Goddess Gaia, who supported the creation of Earth civilization by Alpha, the God of origin.

The Shape of Things in 2100

H.G. Wells Predicts the Future of the World

What does H.G. Wells see for our future today? What was the nature of the crisis and hope he predicted in his novel, *The Shape of Things to Come*? His answers to these questions reveal the importance of bringing change to our world today to bhild a positive future.

For a complete list of books, visit okawabooks.com